GET

WITH
ALVIN HALL

ALSO BY ALVIN HALL

Money For Life
Winning With Shares
Your Money or Your Life
What Not to Spend
You and Your Money

GET OUT OF DEBT WITH
ALVIN HALL

HODDER &
STOUGHTON

To Jillian
for her remarkable and inspiring success
and
To Jonathan
for his growing awareness of the emotional
calm and freedom of living debt free

Copyright © 2006 by Alvin Hall

First published in Great Britain in 2006 by Hodder & Stoughton
A division of Hodder Headline

The right of Alvin Hall to be identified as the Author
of the Work has been asserted by him in accordance
with the Copyright, Designs and Patents Act 1988.

A Hodder & Stoughton Book

1

A CIP catalogue record for this title is available from the British Library

ISBN 0 340 83357 2

Typeset in Berkeley Old Style by Hewer Text UK Ltd, Edinburgh
Printed and bound by Clays Ltd, St Ives plc;

Hodder Headline's policy is to use papers that are natural, renewable
and recyclable products and made from wood grown in sustainable
forests. The logging and manufacturing processes are expected to
conform to the environmental regulations of the country of origin.

Hodder & Stoughton Ltd
A division of Hodder Headline
338 Euston Road
London NW1 3BH

CONTENTS

Acknowledgements

Thanks to the following people for their diligent, thoughtful, and expert work on and contributions to this series of books: Laura Collins (for her brilliant copy editing), Emma Heyworth-Dunn (for her useful initial comments), Helen Coyle (who inherited this project and handled it and me with expert and caring skill, not unlike a midwife), Jonathan Drori (for giving me my first opportunity to do television), Daisy Goodwin (who hired me for *Your Money or Your Life* through which I gained many of the insights in this book), Stephanie Faber (for her expert publicity for my TV show and her ongoing encouragement and friendship), Richard Farmbrough (for being my always honest friend and for his sensitive production skills on the first three series of *Your Money or Your Life*), Emma Longhurst (for her great publicity work at Hodder), Vicki McIvor (for her dedication as my agent, protector, adviser, and friend), Robert McKenzie (for being true blue and generous with his knowledge and opinions), Gill Paul (for her initial efforts in helping to shape these books), Sarah Pennells (for her generosity, expertise, and wry sense of humor), Rowena Webb (for believing in my work and always being honest about it), Karl Weber (for being my trusted friend, my moderator, my spiritual inspiration), and, as always, everyone who appeared on *Your Money or Your Life, Investing for All with Alvin Hall, Save Me, Alvin* and other series I've done. Thanks for making me feel that my work was beneficial. Through these books I hope to share with others my knowledge of the practical strategies, insights, and benefits of handling your finances with focus, discipline, and a little fun. I know that each of you can make your money work in ways that will enable you to achieve some of the things we all desire — a debt-free life, a beautiful home, and the comfort of financial security.

Alvin Hall, London, April 2006

1 | THE WHOLE TRUTH: FACING AND ORGANISING YOUR DEBTS

If you are buying this book, either you or someone you know is having problems, perhaps severe problems, with debt. You are looking for a way out of the financially and emotionally stressful situation in which you find yourself day in and day out. Or you want to give someone you care about – your spouse or partner, your child, a relative or a close friend – a tool that will help them find a way out of their situation and begin to set things right.

This no-frills mini guide is written for the person who needs to face the stark truth of his or her troubling financial situation and who wants to do something about it. In short, the person is ready to take action. Don't expect a magical remedy: I'm no conjurer. Don't expect a totally painless solution: I am no anaesthetist. And don't expect everything to go smoothly: you are human after all. What you can expect from this book is practical and empathetic guidance about getting your debts under control, paying them off and giving yourself a fresh start – this time on the right track. As you make progress, I will also help you cope with and learn how to manage the emotions related to money that will most likely be your greatest nemesis – silent, but always present.

The most important key to getting out of debt, no matter how huge, and staying out is keeping yourself motivated. It will take more effort and discipline – mentally and emotionally – than you can probably imagine at this point. Importantly, do not let yourself focus repeatedly or obsessively on the restrictions that are a necessary part of rectifying your situation.

In the early stages of taking control, your rebellious or contrarian tendencies can seduce you. They will cause you to throw caution – and your money – to the wind. You'll want to say to yourself, 'Oh, sod it!' as you order another glass of wine, buy a new piece of clothing you know you can't afford or write another cheque that will take you even deeper into your overdraft. You might even decide to get another credit card – always 'the last one' – just to get you through another difficult patch. You will know in your gut that you should not do any of these things. But you'll do it just to show that you can, just because it is easy, or just because it makes you feel better at that moment. However, what you are really doing is adding to the frustration and stress in your life.

Keep yourself motivated by focusing on how much better

your daily life will be when your finances are in order and the bills are being paid on time.

- Focus on the progress you are making when you see that the amount of your indebtedness is declining each month. It will probably be slow at first, but over time the speed of your financial recovery will increase.
- Focus on the freedom you will feel when you are, firstly, out of the intense stress of having the debt collectors constantly on the other end of the phone and, secondly, free of all the bad debts that had imprisoned you and severely limited the choices you could make.
- Focus on the time when you will be able to open the mail or answer the phone without dread, go on a holiday that you know you can pay for, or change jobs without feeling such a move is too risky.

This book will help you (or someone you care about) remove the burden of debt. The contents list lays out the seven stages of successful debt recovery. As you read about and begin taking the necessary action, you will undoubtedly notice that I use two voices in the book. These different tones reflect my experience in dealing with people with various amounts of debt. In the early stages, when people are in trouble and want a solution desperately, they want to be told exactly what to do. The voice of a strict teacher is appropriate.

However, as soon as people begin successfully accomplishing some early-stage tasks, they start to feel in control and no longer respond well to finger-wagging. Instead, they want the voice of a companion. This voice enumerates the choices available, helps them evaluate which option is most suitable for them and then supports them as they find and travel on their own path. This second voice acknowledges two important changes that occur in you, the person who is now getting out of debt. Firstly, it recognises that you are making positive steps toward taking back control of your financial life. Secondly, it recognises that you are developing the ability to make better decisions than you did in the past. If you were to trip or encounter some unexpected situation, you now know how to implement the financial restraint that will enable you to recover and continue to move forward.

Many of us make financial mistakes (e.g. taking out a larger educational loan than you really need and using the money inappropriately) and missteps (e.g. spending an anticipated pay rise and then not getting it). But none of us need to be held hostage to those mistakes or to the interest they are costing us every single month. By using this book, one of the helpful organisations listed in it or some other source to help you pay off your debts, you will create your own new beginning. And from this point, you can assemble a different and better financial life for yourself, one that is practical, more effortless and sustainable for your long-term financial well-being, however you define that for yourself.

Stay motivated. Stay focused on your debt-free future. You can do it. And you must do it, for yourself.

Getting Started

Anticipation is often worse than reality, but sometimes it's not. When you're in debt, it's terrifying to think about the big picture. The whole truth and nothing but the truth may cause you to have nightmares about losing your much-loved home, being overwhelmed by huge stacks of unpaid bills or having debt collectors and bailiffs who look like Jack Nicholson in *The Shining* appear at your door. That's why we will begin with a gentle, but no less eye-opening, first step.

This approach is based on something I learned when I was growing up on a subsistence plot of land in the Florida panhandle. Each day we used a hoe to chop the weeds out of what seemed a large vegetable garden to my young eyes. There were so many rows to be weeded that just thinking about the task felt overwhelming. This dread was heightened by the fact that I always knew that once I finished all the rows, I would have to start all over again because the weeds never stopped growing. To get the job done without the frustration, I was given the following advice: 'You can't think about the whole field at once. Just take it one row at a time.' That's what this book will do for you. It will teach you how to remove debt from your life one payment or one negotiation at a time.

As you go along, don't waste your mental energy trying to guess the outcome. It may be that a simple rearrangement of your financial affairs will lift you out of your crisis. Or it may be that more drastic measures are called for. Just take each step diligently and gradually your path to getting out of debt will emerge.

The time it will take you to complete the tasks in this chapter will depend on how organised you've been about keeping track of your financial statements and bills. There are people who throw everything into a dresser or desk drawer, those who get their bills mixed up with the newspapers and 'inadvertently' throw them out with the rubbish and those who get so freaked out that they do not even open any letter that vaguely resembles a bill. No matter how you've dealt with your bills in the past, today is your first step toward a new beginning. It's time to see exactly how much debt you are in. No more 'almost', 'about' or 'around' when you're asked how much you owe. You must know the exact figure.

How Much Do You *Really* Owe?

You'll need paper, pens, a calculator and copies of the tables on pages 8 and 14. (Please enlarge these if you need to.) If you are good at using your personal computer, you can create a spreadsheet for this step. This will certainly make doing the calculations much easier.

Next, get copies of all your outstanding bills, the most recent credit-and store-card statements, loan statements, hire-purchase agreements and any other debt you have. You must include every single debt. Do not forget about money borrowed from family and friends. Unless they have specifically said otherwise, they are expecting you to repay these loans. Also include any council tax arrears, any VAT or income-tax payments if you are self-employed: *all* monies that you owe. If you cannot find a recent statement, call the companies concerned and ask them to send a copy of an up-to-date statement (some companies charge for this) or to give you the specific details you need to complete the spreadsheet. If you share debts with a partner or spouse, he or she should do this exercise with you. It is important to make sure that this person has not taken out any debt in both your names that you do not know about.

Once you have gathered all the information together, fill in the table on the next page. The names provided in the first column are intended to show you the types of debt that must be included. Enter the specific company or person's name in the first column when you fill it in.

At this point, it is important to pay attention to the last two columns. Look at the total for the outstanding

Calculating Your Debt

COMPANY OR PERSON	ANNUAL PERCENTAGE RATE (APR)	OUTSTANDING BALANCE	MINIMUM MONTHLY PAYMENT
Mortgage			
Mortgage on another property			
Second mortgage or home-equity loan			
Student loan			
Credit card A			
Credit card B			
Credit card C			
Store card A			
Store card B			
Bank loan A			
Bank loan B			
Consolidation loan			
Money owed to parents			
Money owed to friends			
Other debts (specify)			
TOTAL			

balance and for the minimum monthly payment. The sight of such a large number for your total outstanding balance may make your situation seem hopeless because you can't imagine when you'll earn enough money to get out from under this massive mountain of debt. If you are like some people who are in debt, this total is probably close to or exceeds the amount that you earn annually from all of your sources of income. (We'll see if this is true later in this chapter.) But do not get depressed or become resigned. Not all debts are equal. There is good debt and bad debt.

Good Debt

Three types of debt are generally considered to be good debt.

Mortgage Loan

This is the debt on the house in which you live and perhaps a holiday home. This is good debt for two reasons. First, it is *secured*. This means it is backed by the value of the property you own. If worst came to worst, you may be able to pay off the entire loan by selling the property. Second, paying a mortgage is considered to be a form of enforced saving. As you are paying off the mortgage capital plus interest, the value of the property should be increasing at a faster rate than the cost of the money you have borrowed. Over time, the increase in the value of the property can provide a substantial return, or profit. This same logic can be applied to a holiday home or flat. However, once a person purchases more than two houses, he or she may be concentrating too large a percentage of their assets in property. This may expose their money to a higher degree of potential loss than is apparent. Remember the old adage about too many eggs in one basket.

Student Loan

A student loan is *unsecured*. This means it is backed only by your good-faith promise to repay it. These loans are a reality of university education because the days when the state could afford to pay for everyone's education are gone – and will probably never return. Borrowing money to pay for one's education is good debt because you are in effect investing in yourself – your professional growth, and your future earning potential. The real problem is that some young people over-borrow on these loans because the interest rates are low. In short, it's a cheap way of borrowing. They then use the extra money to buy a new car, for example, or pay for a nice holiday. Essentially, they use it to pay for a lifestyle, not an education.

Car Loan

Car loans are secured, backed at least in part by the value of the car. Because many people need a car to do their jobs, buying a practical car using a loan is usually considered to be good debt.

(I'm not talking about buying your dream Aston Martin.) Without a car, the person would not be able to get to his or her job and earn money. Buying a second car with a loan is not usually considered to be good debt unless it is absolutely necessary.

Bad Debt

Any and all consumer debt is considered to be bad debt when you cannot afford to pay off the amount in full each month. This would include the holiday that you charged on a credit card four months ago and are still paying for, the presents you bought with a store card and are only making the minimum payments for and the 48-month consolidation loan that you used to get rid of your debts, only to run them up *again*.

By carrying this debt from month to month, you are accruing interest, which adds to the cost for the items you've already bought and used. The higher the interest you pay, the greater the cost. The sources of bad debt are:

- credit cards
- store cards
- unsecured bank loans, including your overdraft
- consolidation loans.

This type of debt is usually the easiest to get when you need it the least. When you have a job and you really don't need the money, you can be flooded with offers for easy credit and loans. You are being seduced. At some point you gave in to the urge to spend tomorrow's earnings today, and soon your spending extends to next week's earnings, then to next month's, even to next year's! Look at the hole you have dug for yourself.

And now when your financial situation could use some help, it is difficult – if not impossible – for you to borrow money at anything but the highest interest rates to help relieve your financial burden. Ironic, isn't it?

What Happens If I Don't Pay a Debt?

The possible consequences of falling behind on different kinds of debt are as follows:

TYPE OF DEBT	CONSEQUENCES OF NOT PAYING
Mortgage	Property repossession and eviction
Rent arrears	Eviction
Loans secured on property	Property repossession and eviction
Council tax	Bailiffs, deduction from wages or imprisonment
Income tax, VAT	Seizures of possessions
Electricity	Supply cut off
Gas	Supply cut off
TV licence	Fine, bailiffs or imprisonment
Magistrates' court fines	Bailiffs, court-ordered deduction from wages or benefits, imprisonment
Maintenance payments	Bailiffs, court-ordered deduction from wages or benefits, imprisonment

| Hire-purchase agreements | Repossession of the goods |
| Credit card, store cards and other unsecured debt | County court judgement against you |

What You Must Focus On

Now that you have itemised all of your debts, do the following calculation:

Grand total of debt owed
− Debt owed on your mortgage
= Debt that you must focus on

This gives you the debt that requires your urgent attention. You can also exclude your student loans if you are not earning enough to have to pay them back. However, if you are earning enough to begin making payments, then do not exclude them from your total. (Note: student loans will be given a lower priority because of the preferential low interest rates charged on them. I will discuss this in more detail later in the book.)

Comparison of Your Debt With Your Income

The next step is to calculate your total annual income. List all the sources and amounts of your income in the table on page xxx or on a spreadsheet created on a computer. Make sure to include maintenance payments, any benefits you receive,

Calculating Your Income

TYPE OF INCOME	MONTHLY AMOUNT	ANNUAL AMOUNT
Salary (after tax)		
Freelance earnings (after tax)		
Partner's salary (after tax)		
Government benefits		
Pension income		
Maintenance		
Investment income		
Rental income		
Other income (specify)		
TOTAL		

income from lodgers, dividends and interest you receive from investments, and all other sources of money that come into (or, more accurately, through) your hands.

If you are in a job where taxes are deducted by your employer, you should list your take-home pay. If you are self-employed and are responsible for paying your own taxes and national insurance, you should deduct the taxes that will be due. Use last year's annual tax bill, or another year's, if the amount you earned was comparable. If such a comparison is not possible, then deduct

25% if the basic-rate tax applies to you or 40% if you are in the higher-rate tax bracket. If you are freelance or self-employed, do not overestimate your income. Be reasonable in your projections. Take an average of your earnings during the last 12 months, making sure there is not an exceptionally high-or low-earning period that will distort the calculation. It is better to be conservative than overly optimistic.

Now it's time to look at the naked truth you've been avoiding. Compare the total of your debt from the Calculating Your Debt table on page 8 with your total annual income shown in the table above. Use the preliminary measures below to evaluate the severity of your situation. Keep in mind the following question: how much of your future have you *really* spent?

- If your total debt is equal to one to two months' salary, you should be able to clear it within one to two years by cutting back on your spending enough to make repayments equal to about 10% of your take-home pay per month. Start thinking about where you can make those cuts now.
- If your total debt is equal to more than two months' salary, you will need to make more drastic lifestyle changes to clear it. We'll explore some ideas in Chapter 2.
- If your total debt is equal to more than six months' salary, it is going to take a huge amount of financial and emotional discipline to repay this. You need to develop a very strict plan for yourself because you will be working to pay off this

debt for years. If you don't think you can do this on your own, seek professional help quickly (see Chapter 7). Don't delay. Understand that these organisations are not there to act as your parent or financial guardian. You must not abdicate responsibility for your debt. These organisations will serve as your adviser or partner in helping you establish, maintain and complete your debt-repayment plan.

At this stage you may still find it hard to grasp and understand the size of your debt and the seriousness of your situation. This has often been the case on my television programme. I understand that it is hard to picture what £10,000, £25,000 or £100,000 of debt looks like. It is easier to feel the stress of it emotionally than to actually see it. On my show, to help an individual or a couple break through their astonishment or wilful resistance, the producers and I would create a visual representation of the debt and its consequences. We've used lots of items – wedding cakes, gold bars, Jenga blocks, chocolates, gold coins and shot glasses. Try the visualisation below to help you get the full picture of your debt and its ramifications on your life.

Gather together some photographs of your family and friends from the last few years. Like most of us, you will probably have pictures from holidays, birthdays, Christmas celebrations and other festive events. There will be pictures of new babies and kids playing in the garden, as well as funny and touching moments that may have faded from your memory. I want you to spread these photos on the floor, laying one next to the other like a mosaic. Lay down one photograph for every £100 you are in debt. A row of ten pictures therefore represents £1,000 of debt. For a debt of £15,000, for example, you will have 15 rows of 10 photographs. (You can change the grid system to fit the layout of your room.) If you have a large amount of debt, you may run out of floor space in the room in which you started. If you do, let your photographs run down the hallways and into other rooms.

When you have laid out all the rows of photographs representing your total debt, stand back and look at all of the people and the moments captured in these images. These are people you love, people who are meaningful in your life. If you are honest with yourself, you will have to admit that they have almost certainly been affected by your money problems in some way. Directly or indirectly, you are robbing yourself and them of happy, stress-free moments like these by not handling your finances responsibly. Maybe some of them have had to bail you out in the past and they remain worried about you. Perhaps your friends have to pick up more than their fair share of rounds at the bar or subsidise you when you've had meals out together or taken a taxi across town.

Are you hiding your debts from your partner? Do you wish your partner would take a more active role in helping you to take control of this problem? Are you still expecting handouts from your parents at a stage when they should be relaxing into their retirement? Could it be that the children in these pictures are learning irresponsible lessons from your example?

Take as much time as you need to think about how your debt is affecting all the people around you and how it will affect the choices you will be able to make in the future.

Do not despair. You have the ability to change a situation that may feel hopeless into something positive. Let the reality you now see clearly, perhaps for the first time, steel your resolve. You don't have to be anyone's victim, especially a victim of yourself. You can make better choices. Say to yourself: 'I can and will get out of debt no matter how long it takes.'

Now gather up your pictures from the floor. Get ready to create a plan of action, including some serious lifestyle and attitude changes that will enable you to free yourself from the burden of bad debt. Make tomorrow the first day in your new financial life. Turn the page and start your next chapter.

Further Preparation

Now that you know what your debts are, this might be a good time to get a copy of your credit report. This will show you how much damage you have done to your credit rating. It will also help you begin to understand how you can repair the damage you have done. Alternatively, you may wish to wait until you have looked at your spending in more detail and implemented a get-out-of-debt plan. We will look at credit reports in detail in Chapter 5.

2 | HOW DO YOU SPEND YOUR MONEY?

Now that you know and have listed the details about each of your debts and have calculated the total of what you owe, your next step is to figure out two things:

1. How you currently spend your money.
2. How much money you can afford to allocate towards repaying your debt each month.

Let's be honest. Both of these are tedious but necessary tasks. You must know clearly where you are spending wastefully so that you can reallocate that money to paying off your debts. The two tasks will take some time and may prove to be a bit frustrating. But you have to complete both of them if you are serious about getting out of debt.

If you are already feeling increased anxiety or the urge to procrastinate and thus avoid completing these tasks, this is the first emotional sign that you need to get a better grip on yourself so you can get a better grip on your money. You have to be your own disciplinarian – as well as cheerleader – if you are serious about getting out of debt and staying there. You must keep yourself resolute for the long road and for the sometimes hard work ahead.

Your Current Spending

Usually I urge people to start taking control of their finances by keeping a spending diary for a month. In it, you would record, *at the same time that you spend the money*, every penny you spend each day. You would also record next to the expenditure what you are feeling at the time or what your rationale is for spending. People are usually astonished at just how much cash can be frittered away on such things as coffees, takeaways, sandwiches, taxis, even careless food shopping.

In this book, however, I am going to assume that you need to take action more quickly. So the first thing I want you to do is work out your monthly spending. Look at your recent bank statements, credit- and store-card bills, mortgage payments, utility bills and other receipts. Reconstruct how you spent all of the cash you withdrew from the ATM over the last 30 days. If they are available, use past bills and receipts to jog your memory. It is important that you be thorough and totally honest. (Note: leave the 'Revised Amount' column on the right-hand side of the table blank. Later, you will enter your revised budget numbers in it.) When an expense is quarterly, divide by four to get the monthly cost. For annual expenses, divide by 12. For the 'Debt Repayments' column, insert the information you calculated and inserted in the Calculating your Debt table on page 8. For the 'Unallocated Cash' column, use the average from the past few months.

Calculating Your Monthly Spending

OUTGOINGS	CURRENT MONTHLY AMOUNT	REVISED AMOUNT
Home		
Mortgage or rent		
Electricity		
Gas		
Water rates		
Council tax		
Service charge		
Telephone (landline)		
Telephone (mobile)		
Buildings insurance		
Contents insurance		
Other (specify)		
SUBTOTAL		

Transport

Car loan
_____

Petrol
_____

Car insurance
_____

Road tax
_____

Public transport
_____

Taxis
_____

Other (specify)
_____

SUBTOTAL
_____

Other Expenses

Life assurance
_____

Income-protection insurance
_____

Private health insurance
_____

Childcare
_____

Maintenance or child support
_____

Pension
_____

Endowments
_____

Other (specify)
_____

SUBTOTAL
_____

Cost of Living

Groceries
_____

Cleaning products and toiletries
_____

Laundry, dry-cleaning, etc.
_____

Medicines and medical costs
_____

Other (specify)
_____

SUBTOTAL
_____

Entertainment

Meals in restaurants

Takeaways

Pub/wine bar

Tobacco

TV licence

Digital TV channels

Internet connection

Books, magazines and newspapers

CDs and music

Cinema, concerts, etc.

Sports/hobbies (inc. club memberships)

Kids' activities

Gambling

Home decorating

Gardening

Antiques and collectables

Other (specify)

SUBTOTAL

Irregular Expenses

Home repairs

Appliances

Car repairs

Pets (inc. vet bills)

Holidays/travel

Christmas gifts

Birthdays and other gifts

Clothing

Toys (for children)

Hairdresser or barber

Other (specify)

SUBTOTAL

Debt Repayments

Credit card A

Credit card B

Credit card C

Store card A

Store card B

Bank loan A

Bank loan B

Consolidation loan

Money owed to parents

Money owed to friends

Other debts (specify)

SUBTOTAL

Unallocated Cash

TOTAL

Recognising Your Financial Imbalance

Compare the total of your monthly spending with your total monthly income, which you added up in the Calculating Your Income table on page 14.

- Does your spending equal or exceed your income?
- What is the exact percentage of your income that you spend each and every month? Do the following calculation:

    Total monthly spending
    ÷ Total monthly income
    × 100

    = Percentage being spent

- If percentages are difficult for you, then do the alternative, simpler calculation below:

    Current monthly income
    − Current monthly spending

    = Money for additional debt repayments

Like most people in debt, you probably already know the answers to these questions and calculations without having to look at the numbers. The calculations let you see the stark truth (as opposed to what you 'think' is the truth) in black and white. If the second calculation yields a negative number, this is the worst possible scenario. You are 'in the red', living and spending beyond your income. You are spending your future earnings before they have been paid to you. Does this make any reasonable sense?

Your challenge must be to determine where you can 'recover' money from your current spending so that you can use it to begin to take better control of your debts and pay them off more aggressively. You can approach this task in two ways:

1. reducing your spending or
2. increasing your income.

Depending on the severity of your financial situation, you may have to work on both of these approaches at the same time.

Reduce Your Spending – Solutions With Immediate Impact

Unfortunately, I can't look over your shoulder as you review your expenses and give you individual advice, so you're going to have to step back and be your own critic and counsellor. Try to imagine what I would say to you. If it helps, pretend there is a mini me watching you with my eyebrows raised, shaking my head and finger slowly. Or if that's too intimidating, think about a relative or other person you know who handles money well and follow his or her example.

Divide your spending into two types: *priority* and *non-priority*. Priority spending includes those expenses you must pay in order to keep a roof over your head, food on the table, the kids in school, lights burning and water running in the bathroom. Go through the long list of your monthly spending and highlight (in colour) or put a tick beside the priority expenses. (I'll talk more about these later in this chapter.)

Non-priority expenses are those items that you spend money on because you *want* to, but you do not *need* to. Do you have to spend £10 each day on lunch at a café near your office? Do you really need to buy a new piece of clothing every week? Did you have to spend the money on a magazine that you could have read at a friend's house? Evaluate each of these items line by line. Think long and hard about whether a particular expenditure is essential. If it is not, think of ways you can reduce it substantially or eliminate it totally. Be strict with yourself.

Here are five top tips to help you quickly reduce your expenses. More complicated ones will be discussed in the next chapter. The tips are also designed to stimulate your thinking about reductions. Don't expect me to give you a complete list of all the changes you could or should make. I am not, after all, sitting right next to you looking at your personal list of expenses. You must come up with some of your own. If you are honest with yourself, you already know where you can make some of these changes. Take ownership of the changes you make.

1. *Cut back on your entertainment expenses.* This is usually the first place most people should look to reduce their spending. Most of us are too casual about both the amount and

frequency of our spending on entertainment and related items – especially on drinks, cigarettes, and restaurants. It does not take long for all of those impulsive £10 and £20 spends to add up to a substantial amount of money each month.

Be realistic and honest about how much you can afford to put in your monthly budget for socialising: £200? £100? £40? And then stick to it. When you go out, take only the exact amount of cash you are permitted to spend. Do not put a credit or debit card in your wallet, because access to additional money may make you vulnerable to temptation. Three glasses of wine can play havoc with your financial willpower. Choose inexpensive restaurants, such as vegetarian, pasta, Indian or Chinese, when you eat out. If you are really broke, organise a pot-luck supper where you ask all your friends to bring a dish or a bottle of wine.

During the week, take packed lunches to work instead of spending £5 on a sandwich or a quick curry. And control your spending on those little sweets and treats throughout the day.

2. *Establish a moratorium on buying new clothes, shoes and other items you already own in quantity.* This is one of the easiest ways to reduce your spending. Go through your wardrobe, your dresser drawer, or wherever you keep your clothing, and ask yourself if you really need more. Do you really need to buy things as often as you do? You can easily stop yourself, if you

really want to, by simply not going into shops and places where you put yourself in the presence of temptation. If you hear yourself saying, 'That's going to be really hard,' it is another clear sign that you need to gain more control of your emotions. You have to see not spending as being more beneficial to your well-being than another item of clothing or gadget.

I'm giving you this advice as a person who loved being a clothes horse but decided that money in the bank gave me much more security than 12 Prada shirts in my wardrobe. During a period when I had financial difficulties, I challenged myself not to buy a new shirt for an entire year – yes, one whole year. It's important to make the period long enough – three months, six months or a year – to be a real challenge for you. I will honestly admit that not buying a shirt for a year, especially my one Etro shirt every season, was a real challenge. In addition to saving, my underlying goal was to make myself think about whether buying that many shirts was a good use of my money. Would I be happier with fewer shirts and more cash in the bank? I re-combined the ties and shirts I already owned to create new, fresh looks, some of which received great compliments from my friends. I would sometimes try on the 'perfect' Etro shirt, but I would never let myself buy it. In each area of my wardrobe, I then limited both the quantity I could own and the price I would pay for a replacement item. For example, I could only buy new shoes if they were 40% or more off and I could only buy a pair when I needed it. No more buying them in every colour available. The positive result was seen and felt in my budget immediately. There was more money available to pay off my debts – and I still managed to look good. I discovered that there is a nice comfort to having more money in the bank. If you are in debt, you will probably find there is greater comfort to watching your outstanding balance decline every month than in spending money you don't have.

3. *Be more careful about the amount you spend on food, especially on takeaways and at the supermarket.* Over the years of doing *Your Money or Your Life* I was always amazed by the amount of money people would spend on food at supermarkets that would eventually be thrown into the bin. They would also pay extra for pre-prepared versions of foods that were easy to make at home. I always challenge these people to radically alter their attitude to food shopping and they usually report that they begin to look at the food in their cupboards and refrigerators differently. They think about what they can do with what they already have, rather than letting it sit there until it's ready to be thrown in the trash. They also find they shop for food more carefully. They think about what they will actually eat during the week, instead of picking fresh foods that are all too often left to become biology experiments in the fridge. By making a few simple changes (like those listed below) in the way you shop for food, you

can recover quite a bit of money from your current
spending.

- Always write out a list of what you need to buy. Plan the
  week's meals so that you don't buy food that will be
  wasted.
- Take a fixed amount of money with you and only spend that
  amount. If your total spend exceeds this amount, select an
  item you can do without and remove it from your trolley.
- Take advantage of seasonal low prices on items like
  vegetables, fruit and other produce. Only buy certain
  staples or basic items (for example, laundry detergent,
  paper towels and cleaning products) when they are on
  special offer.
- Give yourself challenges, like not spending more than £5
  on a bottle of wine. (If you like wine, you'll probably
  enjoy the challenge of trying to find a good one within
  your price range.)
- Reduce the number of pre-prepared meals you eat during
  the week.

4. *Limit the number of instant, 'feel good' expenses.* Cancel that gym
   membership you seldom, if ever, use. Lighten up on buying
   all of those magazines, CDs and DVDs that you read, listen
   to or look at once before they end up crowding the shelves
   in your home and collecting dust. If you smoke, commit to
   reducing the number of cigarettes or stopping completely.
   Avoid laying out cash for items at your favourite DIY store

that end up never being used. Stop yourself from buying another toy or gift for a child who already has so many that the gift ends up in the closet and forgotten about. These are small savings; however, when added together, they can equal one or two extra debt payments each month.

'But sometimes I need a little pick-me-up, a little retail therapy.' This is the response I hear most often to the above advice. And I readily acknowledge that buying something beautiful or tasty for yourself can make you feel better. However, if you need a pick-me-up every week or two, then your spending is probably symptomatic of some deeper problem, such as unhappiness, frustration about your job or relationship, insecurity, the need to feel loved, a sense of entitlement or a form of compulsive behaviour. Rather than using your money to buy what is really a short-term emotional sticking-plaster, resolve the underlying problem and use your money more wisely to handle another problem – your debts.

5. *Limit your withdrawals from the cash machine to one per week.* Taking money out of the cash machine impulsively is one of the easiest ways to fritter your cash away with no record of where it has gone. Most people do not keep the receipts from their cash-machine withdrawals. And even fewer reconcile the amount with their current-account balances.

Set a fixed amount that you permit yourself to withdraw on the same day every week. The amount should be what you would normally expect to spend using cash during the week. You have to be careful with this money, because if you spend it all, you cannot let yourself return to the cash machine until the same day the following week. You will be surprised at how your spending changes as you approach the end of the week and start seeing your cash running low. You automatically begin putting the brakes on your cash outlays. If you are the type of person who cannot carry that much cash in your purse or wallet without wanting to spend it, then place the money you've withdrawn in an envelope and each day take out only the amount you *may* spend. That is all the cash you will carry with you each day.

This situation will force you to be both restrained and creative. (Most people associate creativity with a lack of restraint or control.) Your struggle and the choices you make will be very instructive, providing you with useful self-insights about your relationship with and views about money.

If you have a credit card (or store card), limit the number of times you can use it each week or month. (Weekly is easier to monitor.) Make it a low number, a very low number. As soon as you've used the card the set number of times, remove it from wallet or purse. Try this with your debit card also.

This exercise will help you to realise that you – like most of us – do not have unlimited funds to do with as you wish. It is unrealistic and ultimately financially damaging to think otherwise. We have to make real choices, some practical and some creative, in how we best allocate and use the money we earn to make us content, satisfied and, every now and then, thrilled.

Recalculation

Go through your entries for the Calculating Your Monthly Spending table and, in the column on the far right, write in the new, revised amounts for your future spending. In reality this becomes your new budget. Now, do the following calculation again:

$$
\begin{array}{l}
\quad \text{Current monthly income} \\
- \; \textit{Revised monthly outgoings} \\
\hline
= \; \text{Money for additional debt repayments}
\end{array}
$$

Hopefully you have been able to make sufficient reductions in your expenses, especially the non-priority ones, so that the remainder has increased. If it has only increased a little, you need to make more reductions. Remember, your goal is to recover as much money as possible from your current spending so that you can reallocate it to paying off your debts.

Boost Your Income – Quick Ways to Bring in Some Cash

Instead of fantasising about 'extra' money miraculously coming into your hands, why not make it happen? Increasing my income was the approach I took when I wanted to get out of debt. To be honest, I found this approach was easier than making the really deep cuts in my budget that would have left me feeling too restricted. There was a clear limit to the amount of deprivation I could tolerate. Yet I was willing to work quite hard to bring in additional money that I would only use to pay off my debts. I did not permit myself to spend any of this money on any kind of treat unless I had reached a specific and hard-to-reach goal in paying off my debts.

Here are some quick ways to bring in some debt-reducing cash.

1. *Take a second job.* That's exactly what I did when I had huge debts in my early twenties. I took a part-time job in a department store. I worked all weekends and holidays. I readily filled in for others when they needed to take time off. I used all – every dollar – of the money I earned to pay off my debts. Yes, I did say *all* of the money. Do not use the money to give yourself any treats. Your treat to yourself is getting out of debt.

    I actually enjoyed the work because it was so different from my full-time job and let me use a different set of skills. Look for a job you are likely to find pleasurable and interesting. That's an important key to making the extra job not feel like a burden.

    I've talked to people who have taken jobs being a part-time sales person in a shop or department store, stocking shelves in supermarkets, tidying people's gardens on weekends, working as an assistant to a painter-decorator, teaching computer courses and driving a taxi. They did this in addition to holding a full-time job so that they could get out of debt. Look around for such opportunities. It may feel like a burden at first, but keep in mind that this situation will not last for ever. On the other hand, once you have paid off your debts, working another job is a great way of quickly building up your savings.

2. *Sell anything you own that is not important to you or that you are not using.* Look around your house. There's probably old jewellery, used books, dishes, vinyl records, furniture, even clothing that you don't use or need. Why not turn these items into cash and use that money to pay off some of your debts? This action should be near the top of anyone's list of options when they are in debt. Turning things you no longer want or use into cash is relatively easy. You can hold a car-boot sale, consign items to a shop or sell them on eBay. It's important to be aggressive and unsentimental in selecting the items to turn into cash. Most of the things you sell will be replaceable if you really miss them. You'll be turning your dust collectors into interest reducers. And your place and your life will be less encumbered and look better as a result. Most people discover that once the stuff is gone their lives are simpler. They feel unburdened, which is exactly the way

they will feel when their debts are paid off. The basic approach should be to sell until it hurts – a little. Then you know you've gone far enough.

In Chapter 5 we'll look at other ways to boost your income, but for now implement these changes, then do the recalculation below.

Recalculation
Are you able to get a job *immediately* and apply all of that money to paying off your debts? How much money can you make from selling off some of your possessions? If you can reasonably estimate the amount by which your earnings will increase, then redo your key calculation.

$$
\begin{array}{rl}
 & \text{Increased monthly income} \\
- & \text{Revised monthly outgoings} \\
\hline
= & \text{Money for additional debt repayments}
\end{array}
$$

Hopefully, again, you have been able to increase the amount available to repay your debts. Remember, your goal is to make as much money as is reasonably possible to pay off your debts – even if it hurts a little.

What Numbers Are You Looking For?

The number you are looking for depends on the total amount of your debt, excluding your mortgage. My goal is to help you to escape from the burden of this debt. However, you do need a realistic measure of how long it is going to take. To give yourself some idea, do the following calculation:

> Total debt outstanding (not including mortgage)
> ÷ Money for additional debt repayments
> = Number of months to get out of debt

Why did I not include the money you are already using to pay your debts? Far too many people make only the minimal payments on their outstanding balances. And if you do that, then you will be in debt for a long, long time – maybe for ever.

The chart below shows you how long it would take you to get out of a £4,000 debt that has an average interest rate of 12.90%. (Note: in the simple calculation above, I did not include the interest that is accruing on your outstanding balance.)

MONTHLY PAYMENT AMOUNT	YEARS TO PAY OFF BALANCE
£200	1 year, 11 months
£150	2 years, 8 months
£100	4 years, 4 months
£75	6 years, 7 months
£50	14 years, 10 months
£40 or less	Never

Now ask yourself: how many months do I want to take getting out of debt? That is one of the numbers you are looking for. The second number is the amount of money you need to recover from your expenditures or earn from additional income to make this happen. If necessary, go back to the beginning of this chapter, evaluate your spending once again and make more reductions. You must do it for a better, debt-free financial future.

3 | CREATING A PLAN TO RESCUE YOURSELF

Now that you have determined how much money you have available to allocate to debt repayment, it's time to develop your own personal get-out-of-debt plan. Keep in mind that getting out of debt takes a lot longer than getting into it and can be more difficult. In offering the following plan, I am making two assumptions about your financial situation. First, I assume that you are ready to get out of debt. You have made that commitment to yourself. You are tired of the pressures, the uncertainties and the debilitating effects of this burden in all areas of your life. And second, I assume that you are current on your mortgage payments or rent, utilities, telephone and other priority expenses. If you are not, then you must make sure that these payments are up to date before you begin paying off other debts. It is essential that you have enough money to be able to get to work (in order to generate income), keep a roof over your head and put food on your table.

Prioritise Your Debts by Their Interest Rates

What is the best way for you to use the money you have available to allocate to debt repayment to pay off your current debts? The best strategy is to *always* pay off the debt that is charging you the highest interest first. This is true regardless of the outstanding balance on any of your debts. The reason is simple: every pound of unpaid debt that you carry from month to month costs you the most in real money. In some cases, your minimum payment on this high-interest debt might not cover the total amount of interest that is added to your account's balance each month. Therefore, on next month's bill, you are charged interest on the prior month's interest. If your payment is late, the creditor adds a late fee to your balance. If the build-up of interest takes you over its credit limit, another fee is added. To be blunt: your bad situation is only getting worse. You are in a lose-lose downward spiral.

Using the list of your debts that you created in the Calculating Your Debt table on page 8, reorganise them according to the annual percentage rate (APR) on each card. It is important to use the *annual* rate, not the *monthly* rate that frequently appears on many statements. If you cannot locate the percentage on a recent statement, phone the card issuer and ask them for the information.

Arrange the interest rates in descending order, beginning with the debt that charges you the highest APR. This establishes the sequence in which you will pay off your debts. If two or more debts charge the same APR, the one with the larger outstanding balance must be placed first. It must then be followed by the one with the second-largest balance. Also include in your list the amount of the outstanding balance and the minimum payment amount.

Allocating Your Money

Now that you have prioritised your debts and know in what order you need to repay them, here is how you would ideally allocate the money that you have available to repay them (which we calculated in Chapter 2). I am assuming that the amount available is in excess of the total minimum payments.

1. Make only the minimum payments on all of your debts except the top one.
2. After you've made all the minimum payments, allocate the remaining money to pay off the outstanding balance on the high-interest debt at the very top of your list. The following example demonstrates how to do this. Let's imagine that by the end of Chapter 2 you had managed to 'recover' £460 from your current spending that you would use to repay your debts. When you fill in your chart, it looks as follows:

COMPANY OR PERSON	ANNUAL PERCENTAGE RATE (APR)	OUTSTANDING BALANCE	MINIMUM MONTHLY PAYMENT
Store card A	29.95%	£1,200	£32.00
Store card B	24.95%	£550	£27.00
Credit card A	18.95%	£1,500	£35.80
Credit card B	12.95%	£4,335	£75.20
Bank loan	8.95%	£2,175	£60.40
TOTAL	–	£9,760	£230.40

If you subtract the total minimum monthly payments from the amount available for debt repayment, your remainder would be £229.60 because £460 – £230.40 = £229.60.

If you add this amount (£229.60) to the minimum monthly payment (£32) on the debt at the top of the list, you can allocate a total of £261.60 to your first debt each month.

3. Continue following the two above steps until you have paid off the high-interest debt that tops your list. When the first debt is paid off, allocate all of the money you were using to pay it off to the second debt on the list. Once that debt is paid off, move on to the third. As you continue down this list, you will be paying off each subsequent debt at a faster rate than the one before because more money is going to pay off the debt itself rather interest.

Importantly, the creditors further down the list will remain happy (and off your back) because they are receiving the minimum payments required.

Your Win-Win Gambit: Lower The Interest Rates and Eliminate Those Extra Fees

Now that you have all of the numbers at your fingertips and a strategy in place, make one of the best strategic moves you can to accelerate your debt repayment plan. Call each of your creditors and ask them to lower the interest rate that you are being charged on your outstanding balances. Start with those charging you the ridiculously high interest rates. Also ask them to waive or refund any additional fees they may be charging your account for receiving your payment a day late or being over your credit limit, for example. You can also ask your creditor to freeze the interest charges – i.e., stop charging any interest to your account. Some companies are indeed willing to do this, but usually only for a limited period of time.

Be persistent. Tell the person that you are trying to get out of debt, that you have a repayment plan in place, and that it would help you enormously if the company would lower the rate it is currently charging to your oustanding balance. Ask nicely, and try to avoid being emotional. If the person you reach in the first instance won't lower the rates, then ask to talk to a supervisor and explain your situation to that person. Don't be afraid to go up the management ladder. It may take several transfers to several different people or even multiple phone calls, but eventually you are likely to get someone who is wiling to work with you, instead of against you. Try to persuade them to lower the rates for at least six months or a year, but preferably for the remaining time you have the outstanding balance, as long as you make the payments on time.

Here is the good news – the win-win as I like to call it. Because you already have a repayment plan in place that was originally based on higher interest rates, you already know that you'll be able to make the agreed upon payments at the lower rates on time (maybe even earlier) and therefore keep your side of the agreement. This will keep your interest charges at the lower rate and avoid all of those other fees until the debt is paid off.

Remember that once you've renegotiated the interest rates with the different creditors you will have to refer back to the list of prioritised debts you created earlier in this chapter and re-order them.

If you have transferred some of your debt to a 0% or low-interest credit card, be sure to note in your table the month the introductory period ends. Also record what the new interest rate will increase to at that time. If you do not pay off this debt by that date or are unable to move it to another 0% offer, you will have to reprioritise the debt on your list when the new rate takes effect.

Do not fool yourself or become complacent about debt on which you are paying no interest. It is still debt. Store- and credit-card issuers often have clauses in their credit agreements that give them the ability to change your APR in response to certain events, like a late payment or exceeding your credit limit. Try to avoid such costly surprises while paying off your debts.

4 | STICKING TO YOUR PLAN

Now that you've created your debt-repayment plan, you must work on

1. sustaining your resolve to stick to and accomplish your plan (the focus of this chapter) and
2. reducing the amount of time it will take to pay back your debts (the focus of Chapter 5).

The first goal involves monitoring and keeping control of your spending emotions, while the second involves periodically reassessing how you can use your money more effectively to get out of debt faster.

You don't have to work on both of these at the same time. However, it is important for you to choose which one has top priority. To help determine this, ask yourself what is most likely to cause you to fail: the day-to-day temptations that entice you to fritter money away, or the loss of resolve during the time that you are paying back your debts? Take some time to reflect on what has undermined you in the past. You know (as we all do quietly and privately) the areas in which you are most vulnerable, although you may not like admitting them to yourself. Being honest about your money habits and tendencies will help you to set the correct priorities that will, in turn, enable you to succeed in both the short and long term.

In Chapter 2 you calculated the approximate number of months it will take you to pay off your debts completely, and in chapter 3 you calculated the order in which you will repay your debts. Your ongoing goal during this time is not only to make the promised payments on time; it is also to take control of or eliminate those bad money patterns that got you into trouble in the first place and that may cause you to slip backwards as soon as your situation starts to improve. You already know, from your unfortunate past experiences, that your lack of self-control will eventually – and inevitably – manifest itself in the mismanagement of your finances. Therefore, you must put in place *in advance* some habits or strategies that will enable you to:

1. monitor yourself
2. keep yourself out of temptation's way
3. restore your resolve when you feel yourself weakening and
4. win the battle when you are face to face with your financial demons.

Controlling Yourself – Short-circuiting Your Urge to Spend

Here is a list of seven sayings, thoughts and strategies that have helped people with different financial personalities and amounts of debt mitigate their urge to spend. The list begins with suggestions that can help you manage or overcome the day-to-day temptations that can lead you to betray your plan and, most importantly, yourself. As you move through the list, further suggestions are designed to help you maintain, and if necessary, reinforce, your long-term resolve.

If feel that you are already in control of the daily challenges that you face, start with ideas that are further down the list, those that have a longer-term focus. As you read through these suggestions, select those that are most appropriate for you, given what you have learned while reflecting on your past habits and what you know (and have literally *figured* out, in the previous chapters) about your finances.

Do not feel the need to follow these exact ideas. Adapt them. Change them. Use them to create new ones. The key is to figure out how to make the needed 'trick' work *inside you* each and every time you evoke it.

1. *Ask yourself, 'Do I need this? Do I really need this?' each time you are about to make a purchase.* Just silently querying yourself in this way will, with absolute certainty, cause you to stop, think

and refocus your impulse from the immediate gratification that's in front of your eyes to your longer-term goal – paying off your debts. These questions also help you to prioritise quickly your 'wants' versus your 'needs'. This is a distinction that many people do not like or want to make.

In order for you to be successful in sticking to your plan, you must stay focused on your real financial need to get out of debt (and stay out), instead of losing sight of your goal because of a misperceived 'need' to buy. Use this personal query to help you do this.

2. *Establish a 48-hour cooling-off period before you can make any non-priority expenditures or purchases.* Two good nights' sleep are usually enough to help you – and almost anyone else – quell the urge to spend and to restore reasonable behaviour to the way you handle money. It gives you time to consider whether you can actually afford to spend the money, as well as how are you going to pay for it, without damaging or lengthening your get-out-of-debt plan. Believe me, I know how you feel when you are standing in front of something that will totally satisfy that gotta-have-it itch. It could be a CD or DVD, a pair of shoes, a new shirt, a perfect piece of furniture or a new coat. You think, 'What if it's sold by the time I come back?' Or you say, 'I just know I'll deeply regret it if I don't get it now.' The self-help response you must learn to say to yourself is 'I will get over it!' If you need, say this to yourself repeatedly as

you hang on to the money that you can use more beneficially to reduce your indebtedness.

3. *Compare what you want to buy with things you already own*. I vividly remember going through people's wardrobes during the filming of *Your Money or Your Life*. I would find nine pairs of virtually the same black jeans or five of the same red leather skirts. I still remember the day that I bought exactly the same plates I had purchased six months earlier. I had made the first purchase impulsively and hidden them from myself (and my guilt) in my sideboard.

   Acquiring identical or similar items is common to people who buy compulsively or impulsively. They see. They want. They buy. And it takes them fewer seconds to accomplish these three actions in their minds than it took you to read them. Try establishing a new sequence of actions for yourself: see, want, go home to compare and, finally, think hard before you buy. Anything that helps to put the brakes on your desire to spend is good.

4. *Calculate the number of hours you have to work, given your after-tax income, to pay for the expenditure*. If you have not saved for a particular purchase, then you are spending next week's or next month's income when you put it on your card or use your overdraft to pay for it. You are not using yesterday's saved earnings, but tomorrow's yet-to-be-collected earnings. You are, in reality, spending your future.

   However, it's not only your future income, it's also your

future time. How many hours do you have to work to pay for this probably unnecessary purchase? Do the following calculation:

Cost of the purchase
$\div$ Your after-tax hourly earnings
= Number of working hours needed to pay for the item

Is that purchase really worth two, three or five of the hours that you'll spend working next week or the week after? If next period's pay is already committed to your priority expenses (mortgage payments or rent, groceries, school uniforms, insurance, etc.), then your unnecessary purchases push you even further along your future earnings time schedule. And this, consequently, increases the number of months it will take you to get out of debt.

This calculation makes it very clear who you will be working for each time you overspend or continue to carry unpaid debts from month to month. You are not working for yourself; you are working for your creditors. Instead of using your future earnings to pay off your mortgage, cover necessary living expenses (including holidays and other celebratory events), accumulate savings, pay for education – all things that add value to your life – most of the money will be used to pay interest on debts you've run up or to pay for a piece of clothing that now languishes forgotten in the back of your wardrobe.

Just think: you will be working *for hours* next month to pay for something you bought *in a minute* last month. Before you spend money that you know you shouldn't, think about your future work time. Is this what you really want for all of those hours spent on the job?

5. *Compare the amount you want to spend with a priority expense, like your mortgage payment, rent or utilities.* Do this simple and quick comparison before you are about to whip out your credit card, store card, debit card, chequebook or cash. You know the amount of each month's mortgage payment or typical food bill, for example. You know how much you pay monthly for utilities or car insurance. These are bills you have to pay in order to sustain your life. Do a quick mental calculation:

$$\frac{\begin{array}{l} \text{Amount you are about to spend} \\ \div \text{ Amount of a priority expense} \\ \times \text{ 100} \end{array}}{= \text{Percentage of a specific priority expense}}$$

Is the amount you are about to spend equal to 5% of a priority or necessary expense? 10%? 20%? Or even 50%? Here is an alternative way of thinking about what these percentages mean:

- 5% means if you spend this amount 20 times it will equal one month's priority expense.

- 10% means if you spend this amount ten times it will equal one month's priority expense.
- 20% means if you spend this amount five times it will equal one month's priority expense.
- 25% means if you spend this amount four times it will equal one month's priority expense.
- 50% means if you spend this amount twice it will equal one month's priority expense.

Recollect a moment. Do a mental calculation of how often you spend this amount of money casually and unnecessarily every week or every two weeks. Over the course of a year, how many mortgage payments do you spend on entertainment? Two payments? Three or four? How many utilities bills could you more easily pay? These comparisons are easy to do and will help you to re-establish or keep your financial priorities in their proper order.

Now that you've learned the concept and understand how it works, begin making this comparison each time you are about to spend. As yourself such questions as 'Can I really afford to spend one-tenth of my monthly rent or mortgage payment this way?', 'Why am I not using this money to help get myself out of debt?', 'How can I use this money in the future to create more long-term happiness and security for myself?'

With this new point of view, you can see how your actions

can still undermine your ability to get out of debt and to build a long-term financial safety net for yourself. At the same time, you can see how a little more discipline in your spending can help you to achieve the debt-free goal you have set for yourself.

6.   *When you spend money on a non-priority item, deposit exactly the same amount in your savings account.* This strategy ties your spending and your saving together. Each time you buy a CD, DVD, lipstick, jumper, pair of jeans, an unnecessary toy for your child, a takeaway (when you already have food at home) or anything that is a non-essential item, go immediately to your bank and transfer the exact amount into your savings account. If you can't physically go to the bank, then make the transfer immediately using telephone or online banking. In this age of electronic banking, your excuses for not making the transfer are just that; excuses.

If you are unable to put an equal amount into savings, then you know that you cannot afford to make the purchase. No formulas or elaborate calculations are necessary to do this. It's a simple and surprisingly effective check on your tendency to spend impulsively.

This approach forces you, in effect, to hold a mirror up to your spending. Every time you spend you also see realistically what you can accumulate. Imagine if you did not spend, but saved both the cost of the item and the equal deposit into savings. Wouldn't you be able to get out of debt at twice the rate you are now? And once you've paid off your debts, wouldn't your savings increase twice as fast?

This strategy will also slowly but surely begin to shift how you think about saving. Initially, it will be your spending urges that prompt you to think about saving: 'If I want to spend, then I have to save.' Over time, however, many people find themselves thinking about saving first: 'If I can't save the money, then I can't spend it.' This subtle psychological shift is important. You are beginning to put thoughts of saving *before* thoughts of spending. Thus you are establishing or re-establishing the correct priority for handling money prudently. Saving should always be a first objective and should take precedence over non-priority and needless spending.

7. *Challenge your 'financial discipline' periodically.* This is a method I frequently use to temporarily halt, examine and change a spending habit. I give myself only one challenge at a time, some for longer periods than others. A typical challenge would be to stop buying something for a period of time. The advantage of this approach is that it focuses your attention, in a thoughtful, sometimes creative and corrective way, on a habit that may be a little out of control. I mentioned in Chapter 2 one example, which was to give up buying an item of clothing – such as shirts – for a year. Another example is detailed below. Try to create your own ways as well.

Instead of going out to dinner on Friday or Saturday night,

stay at home and set a limit on how much you will spend on food for the entire meal. This will test your ability to use what's already in the refrigerator or cupboard, your bargain-hunting skills in the supermarket and off-licence, as well as your creativity in the kitchen. How much should your limit be? A good benchmark is the cost of your favourite takeaway meal. If you are really up for the challenge, set your limit at 75% of that amount. Then try gradually decreasing the amount each month until you find your lowest limit. (Personally, I've always found this an interesting and curiously comforting number to know, just in case there's a financial catastrophe in my life.)

Because you are focusing on a single aspect of your spending (or more accurately overspending) during this exercise, you will usually find it easier to be successful at the challenge. It will also be easier to change your perception of the necessity of future purchases. Of the items that you are wearing or using, which ones have proved to be the most satisfying and which ones have been a waste of money? The end result is that you will spend less on fewer items that give you greater satisfaction. This will help you break the cycle of overspending and getting into debt.

If these seven suggestions (and others included throughout this mini guide) fail to work for you or do not spur you to create your own, try asking yourself one question: what would Alvin say? To be honest, there might be times when my response to your debt situation would closely remind you of Faye Dunaway in *Mommie Dearest* when she, playing Joan Crawford, sees wire clothes hangers in her daughter's wardrobe. However, in most situations where people find themselves in debt, I believe they know or sense what is prudent financial behaviour. What most of us want when we are in these stressful situations is guidance as to what we can do, to be pointed in the right direction.

My suggestions are not rocket science. They are closer to plain ol' common sense. However, no one may have ever told you these things. Or you may not have been listening when they were explained to you. Regardless, all of that is in the past. Today, your goal is to use these suggested strategies or your own variations to find the emotional switch inside yourself. It will enable you to control those urges that led you to this point. You will begin to know that you can change things, that you can stick to your plan. And, importantly, you will begin to see and feel the unencumbered lightness of a debt-free life ahead.

Three Reinforcements

1. Encapsulate the strategy you use to contain your spending urges into a saying, philosophy or reminder, such as 'What

would Alvin say?' Write the phrase, sentence or question on labels. Put a label on the front of your credit cards, debit cards or store cards. Print bigger labels and place them inside your purse or wallet so that you see them each time you open it. Place them on your bathroom mirror, on the refrigerator, on the cabinet above the kettle, by the door you use when you leave home, on the back of the visor in your car and on your chequebook. Put them wherever they need to be to remind you of your primary goal – to get out of debt.

2. If you feel you are drifting off your plan but can't figure out why, try keeping a spending diary every day for at least a month. Carry a notebook with you and write down every expenditure the moment you make it. Also record your feelings at the time, especially why you are spending. Review and pay careful attention to your reasons for spending. You may discover that there is an underlying emotional dissatisfaction that your spending is trying to mollify. Confront and resolve the real issue. Stop using spending to repeatedly, and uselessly, put plasters on the symptoms.

3. Schedule a few treats into your self-control strategy and give them to yourself only when you have successfully accomplished your objective. Two phrases are important in this last sentence. The first is 'few treats'. Your real treats are getting out of debt and learning that you can control

your spending. Nonetheless, thoughtfully select a few additional treats that will motivate you toward your goal. The second key phrase is 'successfully accomplished'. Trying isn't enough. Only your success makes you eligible to enjoy your periodic treats as well as the greatest treat – the day you make that final payment on your debts.

5 | IMPROVING YOUR PLAN

Now that you know how to stop yourself from being your own worst financial enemy, you can begin to selectively and strategically extend the ways you handle your financial situation. The repayment plan you have already developed serves as your basic approach to getting out of debt and staying that way. It does not, however, have to remain static. As you begin to feel more confident about both your self-control and your basic money-management skills, you will begin to see other practical approaches that will help you accomplish the next two goals:

1. correcting the damage you have done to your credit rating and
2. reducing the amount of time it will take you to pay off your debts.

Keep in mind that no magic or quick-fix solutions exist. If you try one of the schemes that you may find on the Internet, read about in a newspaper advert or are told about by a friend, the odds are high that you will end up in a worse financial position than before. Your best bet is to stick to your plan at first. Let time, experience and reflection open your vision to changes or tweaks that will make the plan work even better for you, given your changing financial position, as you progress toward freedom from debt. I know this sounds like you have to sit and wait for inspiration or divine financial intervention. You don't. As you are making sure your bills get paid on time and the total amount of your debt is steadily declining, there are other steps you can take to help yourself accomplish the two goals stated above. I'll explain them to you in this chapter.

Get to Know Your Money

'If you take care of your money, then your money will take care of you.' This adage tells us that we have to spend time with our money in order to learn how to use it prudently and profitably. Money, no matter how much you have, does not take care of itself. Think about those people we sometimes read about in the newspaper who one or two generations ago had huge fortunes but are now forced to sell off the family silver, portraits and property because the money has been depleted. No one tended it, either to make it grow or just to sustain its value. The money sits in an account and dissipates – through careless spending, fraud, inflation, ignorance or just plain laziness.

Taking care of your money takes time: time to work through your finances, to balance your chequebook, to pay your bills on time, to read books and articles about money and to listen to TV and radio programmes about personal finance. Take time also to think about how your money can work best for you. By taking time you will be able to develop the practical skills and knowledge you need to make your money work for you. To be blunt, handling money well is quite similar to sex. You have to do it in order to understand the basics, become more insightful about it and better at it over time. Experience is knowledge.

Clean Up the Past for a Better Tomorrow

One of my basic personal philosophies is that you can't change the past, because it's already happened. It is better, I believe, to learn the lessons that the past teaches us and then focus on the future – the part of our lives we can change and make better, using the wisdom we've gained. Unfortunately, this philosophy doesn't quite hold true when it comes to debt. Your past can and will haunt you. The ghosts come in the form of your credit reports.

Most people who are in debt have damaged, even ruined, their credit rating because of missed payments, total defaults, county court judgements (CCJs) or bankruptcy. Each and every get-out-of-debt plan must include repairing your credit report and credit rating. I have heard people argue, somewhat self-righteously, that they do not need to worry about this because they are *never* going to be in debt again. People are usually referring to consumer debt when they say this. However, a bad credit report can cause you to be turned down for a mortgage – a good form of debt – causing that dream house to slip right through your hands. It can also adversely affect your eligibility for certain jobs.

To prevent your past mistakes from taking away your dreams, once you've taken control of the problems and have begun paying off your debts, you should order a copy of your credit report from each of the three reference agencies: Equifax (www.equifax.co.uk), Experian, (www.experian.co.uk) or Call Credit (www.callcredit.plc.uk). It will cost you a small amount of money, but it's well worth it in order to put your past truly behind you. Review all three reports carefully. They may appear complex and intimidating at first because of the amount owed and the small size of the type. Don't be deterred. I promise you, it's easier to understand than it looks. Each company provides relatively clear instructions for deciphering and understanding the information on their reports. You will need patience, both with the report and with yourself, and a comfortable chair to sit in as you review your report. Expect to have some frustrating moments when you will want to throw the report in the bin and walk away. Don't. Make yourself stay there and work on getting through the fog and understanding your report.

There is widespread misunderstanding about what information actually appears in a person's credit report. Popular myth holds that the credit agency puts 'black marks' on your credit report. This belief is false. The reference agency records the information sent to it by your creditors (credit-card and store-card issuers, banks, hire-purchase providers and other lenders). If, for example, you have repeatedly made late payments on your credit card, the issuer of that card reports the details of this chronic lateness (e.g. how many months overdue and the number of times) to the reference agency. When another company to which you have applied for a loan runs a credit check on you, it will see your history of late payments. This could indicate that you are having financial problems or are negligent in handling your money, although the specifics behind the late payments will be unknown to the reference agency. Using its own internal criteria (which includes information that you included on your application), the company to which you have applied for the loan evaluates this information and then may reject your application. So who puts the 'black marks' on your credit report? You do. In reality you, not the reference agency, give yourself a negative rating by missing payments, ignoring bills and handling credit irresponsibly. This is not to say that the reference agencies are never at fault for collecting and disseminating incorrect information or making it difficult (and frustrating) for you to correct the flawed information they have. But the bottom line is that you have to take responsibility for the errors you made, for setting the record straight and for working at improving your credit rating.

What to Do If You've Been Refused Credit

If you are refused credit by a company, write to them within 28 days asking why they made this decision, whether a credit reference agency was used and, if so, which one. They are legally obliged to give you this information. Meanwhile, don't rush to apply for credit from other sources. The reference agencies keep a record of every time you apply for a loan and are turned down. The more often you are refused credit, the more it justifies a creditor's negative decision. This is true even if the original refusal was based on an error.

If the lender replies saying that they did use a credit reference agency, you should write to the agency asking to see a copy of your credit report. Agencies are legally obligated to provide you with a copy of your credit report. Enclose a cheque or postal order for the amount needed to pay for the report with your letter. If you are making your enquiry online, you can use your debit card. (At the time of writing the charge is £2.)

The agency will need to know your full name, address and

postcode, the length of time you've lived at that address and any other addresses you have occupied over the last six years.

Your file will include the following information:

- Your entry on the electoral roll, plus the names of the previous occupants of the property if they have the same or a similar name to you.
- Credit information about any other people who live with you.
- Any court action taken against you: CCJs (called decrees in Scotland), administration orders, IVAs (called trust deeds in Scotland) and bankruptcies (known as sequestrations in Scotland). Debts you were ordered to pay by the court that you paid within a month should not appear. Others that you took longer than a month to pay should be marked 'satisfied'.
- Details of loans and credit cards you've had and whether repayments were made on time. The scoring system should be explained in an accompanying leaflet.
- Any enquiries the agency has received about you from other lenders in the last one or two years (i.e. instances when you have applied for credit).

Go through your reports carefully. Use each agency's leaflet or online explanation to help you understand the information.

What to Do If You Spot a Mistake

If anything is factually incorrect in the reports, you can correct it. You should either contact the lender directly, or go through the credit reference agency, which most people choose to do. Write to the agency telling them what's wrong and enclose supporting documents if you can. For example, if their records erroneously show that you did not repay a bank loan, send them a copy of the final statement or a letter from the bank or company you received when the debt was satisfied. If you are correcting the information online, follow the instructions on the website carefully. Be succinct, clear and brief in specifying how the information is incorrect and why it should be corrected. You may find it daunting and frustrating, in particular if you are trying to correct some of your information online. It may make you angry. Be diligent. Remember you are doing this ultimately for your long-term financial benefit.

Since the reference is based only on your name and address, it is not altogether uncommon for mistakes to be made. If your name is Moira Templeton and the previous occupant of the house was Maurice Temple, you could be taking the blame for Maurice's misdemeanours. If your ex-partner has the same surname and initials, that's asking for trouble. Cases of mistaken or confused identity do occur and it's important to clear them up, no matter how time-consuming the process might be.

Whether you choose to clear up mistakes in your credit

report by letter or online, it will take time and patience – lots of patience. Always communicate with the credit reference agency and your creditors *in writing*. It is very difficult to correct errors over the phone. If something goes wrong, you will end up in an 'I said, you said' argument. And, let's be honest, given the unfortunate information that already appears in your credit report, your credibility is already compromised. It is imperative that you have a paper trail of your correspondence and conversations just in case you need it.

Your Ex and a Notice of Disassociation
If your credit rating is being adversely affected by the behaviour of a former partner (business or romantic), you can have a *notice of disassociation* attached to your file, stating that they no longer have anything to do with you. Avoid emotive language in your notice. It should be clear, straightforward and present only those facts that are important to your creditor. Here's an example:

> Ms Irene Smith wishes it to be made clear to any potential lender that the information in the name Mr Ray Sullivan relates to a former partner with whom she shared a rented home and joint account until April 2005. Any further information in Mr Sullivan's name has no connection with Ms Smith. Ms Smith stresses that she holds no responsibility for any accounts in Mr Sullivan's name and requests that anyone searching this file takes this

into consideration when evaluating an application for credit from Ms Smith.

What Happens Once I've Sent a Correction?

When you contact the credit reference agency about a mistake, the information will be flagged up as 'disputed' and lenders will be warned not to rely on it. The credit reference agency will contact the lender on your behalf and the lender has 28 days to reply to the agency. In information is amended as a result, a new copy of your credit report will be sent to you free of charge.

If they refuse to make the correction you suggest, or don't reply, or the information is factually correct but does not reflect your circumstances, you can write your own note of correction and ask them to attach it to your file. It shouldn't be too long – not more than 200 words. (They don't need to know the full saga of your financial problems.) It's a good idea to add a note of correction if there's a specific reason why you defaulted on the loan, for example if you suffered an injury and couldn't work for a while, if you were made redundant or got divorced.

Review Your Report Regularly

It is a good idea to review your credit report periodically (annually is generally suggested) to make sure it remains accurate. Also, if you have been subject to some type of identity theft involving your credit, the first sign of it may appear in your credit report. It's worth the few pounds every year to avoid such nasty little surprises popping up on your record and the consequent unnecessary hassle or financial difficulty.

What to Do to Improve Information That Is (Unfortunately) Correct

There is only one way to correct a bad credit report that is accurate and correct about missed payments or late payments: immediately change your behaviour and start making your payments on time. As you continue to do so, your credit rating will gradually improve. However, don't expect that to happen overnight; after all, it took you some time to get yourself into this situation. I think it's a good idea to monitor your credit reports regularly when you are trying to improve your rating. Seeing your situation get better can motivate you during what will sometimes feel like a long – and slow – effort.

If you have had county court judgements (CCJs) or filed for bankruptcy, get guidance about the ways to improve your credit report by doing research on the credit reference agencies' websites.

Here are some guidelines to follow to help you deal with a poor credit report:

1. Remember to always deal with your credit reference agency in writing.
2. Follow the instructions and guidelines provided in the

frequently asked questions (FAQ) on each website. They cover a wide range of topics related to your report and improving your credit rating. Below is a partial list of subjects covered at the FAQ section of Experian's website:

- What should I do if I can't pay my debts?
- Are there any organisations that can help me with my debt problems?
- Can I get other people's financial information removed from my credit report?
- Can I explain my circumstances on my credit report?
- If I make a query about specific information on my credit report, when can I expect an answer?
- What do credit repair agencies do?
- How can I improve my chances of getting credit?
- Can I have a copy of the new credit report when it has been updated?
- Can I find out who has searched my credit report?
- I've paid a judgement. Why is it still on my credit report?

The reference agency websites offer examples of letters (see the sample below from the Experian website) that can be used to create your own correspondence.

The examples given are usually clear and to the point. Make your life easy; use them as your guideline instead of trying to create your own. It will help the agency to help you more easily. Remember, you are not the first person to be in this situation, and the agency has lots of experience in helping people correct and improve their credit histories.

3. If you have to speak with a customer service representative of one of the agencies over the phone, be nice. Try to avoid being confrontational, nasty or cynical, although I can easily understand the frustration that can lead to such behaviour. When the rep feels you are a nice person, it is more likely that he or she will work with you instead of wanting to do nothing to help you. Remember the old adage about winning people with kindness.

Credit-repair Agencies

Bad credit is a huge stumbling block in anyone's progress toward the financial and material goals you have in life. It is definitely a problem nobody wants in his or her life. And it is one that every person who has encountered it would be thrilled to have someone else solve, to make it just go away. Those advertisements from companies offering to repair your credit in return for a modest fee can seem like the deliverance you need from the problems caused by bad credit. The logic is simple: you pay the money and the company makes your problem disappear. Well, it's not that simple. There are no advantages to using a credit-repair agency. They don't have any special bargaining power with the credit reference agencies or your creditors. So what's the point of paying a fee to someone else to do something you can do just as well yourself? It just takes time and diligence. And if you repair your credit yourself, I'll guarantee you will learn all of the lessons you need to avoid ever letting yourself get into the bad-credit miasma again.

Paying Off Your Debt Faster

As you are working on improving and correcting your credit report, you should also be thinking about ways to pay off your debt even more quickly. The faster you pay it off, the sooner you can put your period of irresponsibility behind you and move on to a lifestyle in which you handle your money in a more thoughtful, targeted way, and with much less stress. I'm always reminded of what a friend said to me after he had put himself on a plan to pay off his debts (which consisted mostly of university loans and credit-card debt) and 'to spend more quality time' with his money: 'I never imaged that being organised about money would reduce some of the stress in other areas of my life. Until now, my money problems were always in the back of my mind like a dark shadow that I was trying to avoid, although I did not admit this. Now that shadow has disappeared because I'm in control.'

Creating ways to pay off your debt faster will indeed make

the shadow go away sooner. Be prepared to sacrifice some of your time. But don't think of it as a sacrifice. Instead, think of it as giving yourself a life in which your financial dreams are again unclouded by your past problems. In Chapter 2 I touched on two of the biggest ways to boost your income – taking on a part-time job (in addition to your full-time job) and selling some of your possessions. Now I want to look at other strategies that will help to bring in some more cash and restrict your outgoings. Even if you don't actually implement the suggestions below, use them as a basis for creating a faster debt-repayment programme of your own with which you are comfortable and that motivates you.

1. *Get a flatmate or rent out a room in your house.* In most people's budgets, housing is the largest expense. Reduce that cost – and allocate the money you save to paying off your debt – by getting a flatmate or, if you own your own home, rent out a room. The government will not tax for the first £4250 of the money you earn from renting a room. (Further details are available on the Revenue and Customs website – www.hmrc.gov.uk.) Keep in mind that this arrangement is only temporary. You will only have to share your space until you get your finances stabilised enough so that you can afford to live by yourself and pay bills and debts. For some people (and I am one of them), this type of arrangement would be difficult. I like living by myself, perhaps a bit too much. If

sharing your space would be too difficult, then do what I did: try one of the other options.

2. *Allocate one day's earnings each week to paying off your debts.* 'I want to pay off my debts, Alvin,' you say, 'but there is one problem: where am I going to get the money?' The first place you can get money is from your own earnings. Allocate one day's earnings each week to paying off your debt. If you are a couple, then both of you should do this.

As soon as you get paid every week, every two weeks or monthly, write a cheque for the appropriate amount of money and mail it to the creditor at the top of your list of debts. By allocating one day's earnings each week, you are indirectly doing something you probably say you can't do: imposing a budget on yourself. You immediately begin living on only four days' income. And as long as you don't use your credit cards and overdraft, you will be surprised how easily this little trick can work. And once your debts are paid off, this is also an easy way to set aside money for savings.

3. *Use any lump sums (like a bonus from your job, an unexpected inheritance or windfall) to negotiate with your biggest creditors.* You may wonder whether your creditors will negotiate. The answer is yes. And there's a greater likelihood of having some negotiating power when you come into a lump sum if you have already established a (new) pattern of regular, on-time payment. Call up your creditor and offer them the entire lump sum in exchange for reducing the amount you owe. Explain where this sudden

ability to pay came from. Let's say you have £6,000 of debt on a credit card. If you get a bonus of £5,000, call up the company and offer them your entire bonus in exchange for wiping away the entire debt (all £6,000) at one time. You not only get £1,000 of debt relief, but think of all the interest you'll be saving that would have built up on that debt. As odd as it may sound to you, some companies will accept your lump-sum-payment terms. This kind of offer can be attractive to companies because they get their money immediately, and they eliminate the risk that you might default over the long term. If the company agrees, make sure you write a letter to the person with whom you made the agreement summarising the specific details *before* you mail that cheque.

4. *Consolidate your debts*. After you've stuck to your original plan for at least six months or a year, there will likely come a time when you have sufficiently shown that you can meet your promised payments and have cleared up enough of the negative information on your credit report. You might be able to consolidate the remainder of your debts. You can do this by moving all of the debts to one 0% or low-interest-rate credit card (if you qualify for one) or getting a consolidation loan from your bank. Hopefully this will not only lower your payment but decrease the interest rate you are being charged on the outstanding balances. The fewer companies, stores and banks you owe, the easier it is to allocate more money to paying off each one. Having said this, I strongly

advise against using debt-consolidation companies. See my advice on page 80.

5. *Consider downsizing your entire life temporarily to get yourself back on track.* Consider selling your house or moving out of the place you rent into one that is more affordable. For many people in debt, this is a hard step to take and a difficult emotional reality to accept. What makes doing this so hard? It is the loss of dignity, pride, face and status. Here it is important to remember that in all areas of our lives sometimes we have to be willing to take quite a few steps backward in order to move forward more positively in the long run.

When a person finds his or her back up against this final wall, it is hard not to feel like a loser. You have placed yourself in the position of having to sacrifice what is probably your biggest asset and strongest emotional tie other than your marriage or your children. I propose looking at the decision to sell in a different way. See it as giving yourself an opportunity to reinvent yourself, an opportunity to start over on a new path with more practical wisdom and self-awareness under your belt. Selling your property and moving to something more modest for a few years allows you to relieve some of the stress of sustaining what is clearly no longer sustainable. Sell the house. Downsize your life for a period of time. Remember what it was like to enjoy the simple pleasures of life before you got caught up in thinking that the only pleasures you could enjoy or wanted to enjoy had to be paid for with increasing amounts of borrowed money. Use what you have learned about money – and yourself – to rise again, like a wiser financial phoenix from the ashes of your burned credit cards, charred credit reports and singed self-image.

A Few No-Nos

In desperation, people can, and often will, make money decisions that further complicate, rather than improve, their financial situations. Here are some common mistakes that can not only cost you more in interest, but can also create more problems in the future.

1. *Don't turn unsecured debt into secured debt.* Another way of saying this is don't refinance your house (which is secured debt) in order to pay off your store- or credit-card debt (which is unsecured debt). Yes, I know you will be paying a lower interest rate on the debt. Yes, I know it will get rid of the debt that is causing you sleepless nights. But I also know how easy it is for that relief from the pressures of debt to transform itself, somewhat like a virus, into something different – a desire to spend. Because the old debt is suddenly 'out of sight and out of mind', people who are

spenders can easily begin justifying how they can use their credit cards 'just a little bit'. And soon a little bit turns into a lot and the debt is back at its old level. They've trapped themselves again in the same cycle.

There are also other reasons not to fold your credit-card debt into your mortgage. Consider how long you'll be paying that mortgage and how much interest you'll be paying on the debt you've hidden from yourself. Additionally, if you think of a mortgage as a form of long-term enforced savings, then by folding your unsecured debts into your mortgage, you just spent part of your future savings – the money that could have been used for your retirement, for example.

2. *Avoid those companies that offer to restructure your debts.* Debt-consolidation companies promise to deal with your creditors for you and reduce your repayments to one single affordable monthly sum. If you're feeling intimidated by dealing directly with your creditors, it can be very appealing to think that a parental figure will take control of the situation for you and act as a buffer. You think that your 'parent' will take phone calls that you don't want to, organise your debts, negotiate with your creditors, make everything easier for you. After all, this company knows loads more about finance than you do. It seems like an easy, painless solution. As tempting as it may be, don't take your debts and stretch them out to 48 months (4 years), 60 months (5 years) or 72 months (6 years).

The lower payments may 'feel' better, but the lengthened repayment schedule just means that you'll still be paying interest for that jumper after you've given it to a charity shop, for that expensive holiday or for that pricey meal for a friend's birthday that no one remembers clearly because you all drank a tad too much. It's best to arrange the debt consolidation yourself. It will take some time, but by sacrificing a little today, you give yourself a quicker debt-free future.

This chapter contains two critical messages about getting out of debt and staying out. First, you must work diligently and patiently to repair the damage you've done to yourself and your credit rating. And second, you must put the debts behind you as quickly as possible by doing everything you can to accelerate the pace of your debt-repayment plan. The good news is that because you will be working on both of these goals at the same time, there will be little time to think about spending. And when you do think about spending, you'll be reminded of the pattern of financial irresponsibility that you are trying to release yourself from and planning never to repeat again. Stay focused on your debt-free future.

6 | WHEN WORST COMES TO WORST

Most people can work out a plan to repay all of their debts. It will often take more time than they would like, and it will mean exercising a great deal of self-discipline – more than they have ever imposed on any aspect of their lives, especially their money. It's discipline that is the most difficult. In some cases, there is actually enough money to get out of debt, but there just isn't the willpower or commitment to see a plan through. For many people who find themselves in financial trouble, it is easier to let themselves be victims of whatever forces they rationalise as being the culprit than to corral themselves and their emotions on to a proactive path that involves discipline, prudent behaviour and making responsible choices.

You, however, may be a person who has the fortitude and the honest desire to make it all right, but you really don't have the money or the possibility of making the money. You look at your pile of bills and statements; you look at what you're able to pay;

you think through again and again all of your options and the efforts you have made to lift yourself out of a worsening financial situation; and you suddenly realise that indeed you are trapped. You've tried debt counselling services. None of your creditors are willing to give you another chance. (You have probably already used up your second and third chances.) At that moment, it always feels as if there is no way out.

Fortunately, even in desperation, with your back up against a wall, you do have choices. There is not just one way to begin putting your overwhelming debts behind you and begin a new, more modest and realistic financial life; there are several ways. None of the choices are easy. In addition to dealing with the courts and financial issues, you'll also have to deal with your personal disappointment, shame and loss of status. Emotionally this will not be easy. Financially it won't be easy. Dealing with the bureaucracy won't be easy. The key to getting through this difficult period is to know that the actions you are taking will give you some immediate relief and eventually give you a chance to start over – hopefully smarter, wiser and more realistic about how you should use your money.

I must be prudent here and emphasise that you should take these steps only after all others have been exhausted. The negative impact on your credit rating and 'credit worthiness' will be immediate, severe and can follow you for some years. But remember that over the long term you can earn back what you have lost, and this time you'll know how to better hang on to your money and your self-worth.

Administration Orders

When you take out an *administration order*, you ask your local county court to deal with your creditors on your behalf. You then make a single weekly or monthly payment to the court (usually by having the money automatically deducted from your regular earnings), and the court distributes the money among your creditors. Administration orders are only available to people who already have at least two separate debts and at least one county court judgement (CCJ) against them and whose total debts are no more than £5,000.

To get an administration order, you have to fill out an application form (N92) that is available from your local county court. You will then have to appear in court, where the judge decides whether to grant it or not. Your creditors will have been informed that you have applied for the administration order and given 16 days to object. Once the order is in place, the court (or an officer of the court) will examine your financial statements and decide for themselves what you can afford to pay. The money will then be taken from your wages or benefits without you having a choice in the matter. The court will take a percentage (usually

10%) of each of your repayments to cover its administrative costs. The order will be listed on the Register of County Court Judgements and reported to the credit reference agencies. Your credit rating will be negatively affected.

An administration order has some notable advantages and disadvantages. The advantages are 1) debt collection letters will stop coming through the post, 2) your creditors must stop charging interest on your outstanding debts and cannot take any other action against you and 3) if your debts can't be cleared in three years, or a 'reasonable period', you can apply to pay what you can during this time and request that the remainder of your debts be written off at the end of the payment period. (Note: a *composition order* is a variation of an administration order that can be used if your debts can't be paid off in three years. In this case, you make payments the same way, and at the end of the period your remaining debts are automatically written off. You don't have to apply to have them removed. You can apply for a composite order at the same time as an administration order.)

The disadvantages of an administration order generally have to do with giving up control of your finances to the courts. Still, it is worth applying for an administration order if you feel that with the help of the courts you can avoid going bankrupt – a much worse choice.

As your financial situation changes, you must notify your court administrator. If, for example, you are not able to make the required regular payments, then you can apply to the county court to have the order changed. If, however, you do not honour the terms of the administration order by failing to make your regular payments, your creditors can pursue you for the whole amount outstanding, even if you have a composition order. As a result, you may be subject to many of the same restrictions as a person who has been declared bankrupt.

Individual Voluntary Arrangements (IVAs)

Individual voluntary arrangements are often a debtor's last alternative before bankruptcy. This is less costly and less professionally restrictive than bankruptcy. (A person who has been declared bankrupt cannot hold certain jobs.) While the total fees are usually lower, the actual costs involved in applying for an IVA can run to several thousand pounds and make this option appropriate if you have unsecured debts of £15,000 or more.

An IVA is a formal agreement between a person in debt and his or her creditors to pay off all or a percentage of the total money owed, usually over a 3–5-year period (30–60 months). Some IVAs are set up so that you can use a lump sum rather than monthly payments, of a mixture of the two, to pay creditors. Because in most cases you will be paying off only part of the total debt, the amount of the monthly payment is less than it would be on all that you owe. A reduced monthly payment is one of the advantages of an IVA. It takes some of the pressure off you and your money. At the end of the period when the IVA has been in effect, any unpaid debt remaining is written off by your creditors.

Because an IVA is a formal, legally binding agreement, you will need to find a licensed insolvency practitioner (typically an accountant or a solicitor) to draw up the document. (Look under 'Insolvency' in the *Yellow Pages* or go to your local county court, which will have a list of those in your area.) All practitioners charge fees for their services in helping you to create your individual voluntary arrangement. Some take their fee out of your monthly payments. Others charge upfront fees. Regardless of how it is paid, this money will come out of your pocket. This licensed professional will help you pull together the documentation required for the IVA. These will include your bank statements, income (at least three months of consecutive pay slips for you and your spouse), assets (property valuation, endowment surrender value), liabilities (mortgage statements) total debts (creditor statements), other expenses and a statement explaining the reasons for your financial difficulty. This last item is very important. The likelihood of your creditors accepting your proposal will undoubtedly improve if the truthful reason for your financial problems is something the people evaluating the proposal can understand or empathise with. The amount you will pay under the terms of your IVA will be based on your disposable income, and it should be an amount you can realistically afford to pay each month. Once you and the insolvency practitioner determine this amount, the practitioner will draw up the IVA proposal, which you should read carefully and then sign.

At the same time, the practitioner will apply to the courts for an *interim order*. If granted, this order prevents creditors from taking further action, like forcing you into bankruptcy, until they meet with you and the practitioner to vote on the terms of the IVA. Before this meeting, the practitioner issues an opinion to your creditors about the arrangement. Most of a consumer's creditors will not actually attend this meeting. Leading up to the day of the meeting, most will vote either by email, fax or post to accept or reject the arrangement.

An IVA can only be approved if creditors representing at least 75% of the total outstanding debt vote for the proposed arrangement. Your creditors may request modification in the arrangement in order to vote in favour of it. If any of the creditors don't vote, it is assumed they would vote for the IVA. Once it's accepted, the IVA is binding to all of your creditors, whether they voted for or against it. Interest stops accruing on all of your debts.

If, however, a creditor representing more than 25% of the debt votes against the IVA, then it fails. A new proposed IVA can be put forward to the creditors. They may want more of your money and net worth, such as the value of any endowment policies or part of the equity in your home, included in the IVA in order to accept the agreement. This would mean that these and other assets could be at risk.

Once approved, the insolvency professional is responsible for monitoring and supervising the plan to make sure that all parties adhere to the terms of the agreement. This means you will no longer have to deal directly with your creditors. This will certainly take some of the pressure off you. Each month you send your required payment to the practitioner. After receiving it (and deducting any fees as specified in the IVA), he or she will distribute the money to the creditor under the terms of the agreement, usually on a pro-rata basis.

While an IVA offers relief from the stress of dealing direct with your debt collectors and lowers your monthly repayments, it still damages your credit rating. During the term of an IVA, you will find it difficult, if not impossible, to get credit of any kind without the permission of your insolvency supervisor. If you do manage to get a loan or credit, you will be charged a higher interest rate, and if it is a mortgage, you will be required to make a larger deposit.

About three months after you've completed your IVA, you will receive a *statement of completion*. Remember any remaining unpaid debts will be forgiven by your creditors. You would be officially free of debts and could make a new financial start. It is up to you, not the practitioner or your creditors, to send this statement to the credit reference agencies to show that you've satisfied the arrangement and to have this information recorded in your credit report.

Failure to keep to the terms of your IVA can be devastating. Having violated the terms of this legal agreement for whatever reason, your creditors can force you into bankruptcy.

In Scotland, an IVA is called a *trust deed*. The details of a proposed trust deed are published in the *Edinburgh Gazette*, and creditors have five weeks to object if they don't want to accept the terms. If they don't object, they are considered to have agreed. A trustee administers the terms accepted by the creditors. The main disadvantage is that creditors who don't accept the terms are not bound by it, and they can still apply to the courts to force you into bankruptcy if you have not been honest or acted in good faith in making your offer. Otherwise, the advantages and disadvantages of a trust deed are the same as for an IVA.

If you have been trying on your own to reach an agreement with your creditors but have reached an impasse, then an IVA is probably your best choice if you want to avoid the complications and costs of bankruptcy. Yes, it will cost you money. (Getting out of debt is rarely free.) However, you will only have to deal with the insolvency practitioner instead of all of your creditors, your required monthly payments will be lower, and you will maintain some control over some of your assets, like your house, while your creditors have the security of knowing that the insolvency practitioner will ensure they will receive regular monthly payments of at least part of the money they are owed.

Bankruptcy

Bankruptcy should only be seen as the last and final option when all other options have failed. You should have diligently and honestly worked with the Citizens Advice Bureau (CAB), the Consumer Credit Counselling Service (CCCS) or other reputable organisation to find a workable solution. You've sought the advice of your bank manager, a qualified account, a licensed insolvency practitioner or other financial professional and have been unable to reach a compromise agreeable to everyone. In short, you have no other choice.

Bankruptcy will seriously affect your 'credit worthiness', your financial life and, in some cases, your professional life, not only for the term of the bankruptcy but for years afterwards. Again, only consider bankruptcy if you can see no other way out of your debt. Make sure you read up about it. (Visit the Insolvency Service website, www.insolvency.gov.uk, for detailed explanations of bankruptcy and your possible alternatives.) Know what to expect. And be prepared to live with the consequences. Frankly, you are handing over control of your financial affairs to others who will make all the choices for you. Control is no longer yours.

If you are considering bankruptcy, don't go on a spending spree in the weeks or months beforehand, running up huge debts in the belief that you will be able to blithely walk away from them in court. The judge's decision will be based on the evidence and his or her sense of your financial behaviour in the time leading up to going bankrupt.

While bankruptcy may appear to be the ultimate resolution to the stress caused by overwhelming debt and financial problems, I think it is important to be aware of its disadvantages. Remember getting out of debt is rarely free of costs or consequences. To paraphrase a favourite saying of one of my oldest friends: everything costs something – either from your wallet, your life or your heart.

- You lose control of all your assets. A court-appointed trustee or official receiver makes all of the decisions about what will be sold to meet your debts and what you are allowed to keep. This means that you could lose your house and your car.
- You are required to disclose that you are bankrupt if you obtain credit of £500 or more, either alone or jointly. You do not have to tell the trustee in advance that you are applying for this credit.
- If you are allowed to stay in your home, a lien (or charge) will be put on it so that your creditors will be entitled to receive some or all of the increased equity when it is sold. Any valuable household items such as expensive electronic equipment could be sold although clothing and furniture will not be.
- You will be required to keep up payments on any mortgage

or loan secured on a property. These debts do not disappear when you are declared bankrupt. Other debts that remain include maintenance payments, court fines, debts obtained fraudulently and student loans.

- Your career and professional standing may be affected. If you have been declared bankrupt while you are working as a solicitor or chartered accountant, you will no longer be able to practice. Bankruptcy can also affect your career if you are in the armed forces or police and you will not be able to act as a school governor, justice of the peace, MP, or MSP.

- If you own a business, it will have to be closed when you are declared bankrupt although you may be able to continue trading on a self-employed basis. During the period of your bankruptcy, you will not be able to start a new business and you will find it very difficult to do so afterwards. Also, you will be unable to serve as a company director or be involved in promoting or managing a company.

- If you come into any money, such as an inheritance or a bonus at work during the bankruptcy period, that money will be seized by the receiver and used to satisfy your creditors. If you earn more than the court deems strictly necessary for modest day-to-day living during the period of your bankruptcy, you will be ordered to pay a percentage of it to the receiver.

- Not only will your bank, building society, insurance company, pension company, utility company, local authority and all of your lenders be notified in writing, but your name and notice of your bankruptcy will be published in the *London Gazette* as well as local and/or national newspapers.

On the positive side, if you have been struggling for a long time to climb an insurmountable amount of debt, are continually being harassed by your creditors, are devoting a huge percentage of your monthly income to paying off your debts and each month only watch them get bigger and bigger, then bankruptcy will be like a breath of fresh air, albeit a very chilling one.

In 2004, the government reduced the term of most bankruptcies to a maximum of a year, rather than the two or three years that were previously the norm. This, in effect, means that it is easier for people who have been declared bankrupt or been forced into bankruptcy to pick themselves up, dust themselves off and start over.

If you have to declare bankruptcy, do not spend lots of time feeling guilty or ashamed. Remember that many people have had to take this step, and not just because of overspending. One common situation that can lead to bankruptcy is when people start a new business by giving personal guarantees to banks and other institutions to obtain loans. If the business fails, then they are personally liable. You could also be forced into bankruptcy if someone takes a high-stake legal action against you and wins, or if you are exposed in ultra-high-risk investments like some of the investors in Lloyds. I'm not saying that some bankrupts aren't reckless profligates. However, it is important to be aware that not all bankrupts are the same.

How to Go Bankrupt

You can file a bankruptcy petition yourself, or any creditor to whom you owe more than £750 can petition to have you declared bankrupt. In the latter situation, you will receive a statutory demand in the post warning you that this is about to happen and giving you a last chance to suggest a compromise or propose an alternative. If you don't respond, the matter will go before the courts and a judge will decide whether issuing a bankruptcy order (which declares you bankrupt) is appropriate.

To petition to have yourself declared bankrupt, you fill out a form that you can get from your local county court, which has jurisdiction in bankruptcy cases. (You can also download the form from the Insolvency Service website, www.insolvency.gov.uk). You will have to pay certain fees when the petition is filed in court. The two most significant costs are a court fee (currently £150) and a deposit (currently £310) to cover administrative costs associated with handling your bankruptcy. Personal cheques cannot be used to pay these costs. You don't have to pay the court fee if a creditor is seeking to make you bankrupt or if you are on a low income or benefits.

The court can either issue a decision regarding your petition immediately or it can schedule a time to consider it. The judge will almost certainly issue a bankruptcy order, at which time you will be immediately bankrupt; but there are other possibilities:

1. The judge can stay the proceedings, indicating that the court would like to get more information before making a final decision at a later date.
2. The judge can dismiss the petition. This usually occurs because the judge believes that another resolution is more appropriate.
3. The judge can appoint a licensed insolvency provider. As I mentioned earlier, the court is obligated to consider whether an individual voluntary arrangement would be more appropriate. If the judge determines that it is, then he or she will appoint an insolvency practitioner. This option is enforced only if the debtor has unsecured debts of £40,000 and assets worth at least £4,000.

After the judge issues a bankruptcy order, you'll be given an appointment or, more likely, a telephone interview with the official receiver, to whom you must give all details of your financial life. This must be done within 21 days of having been declared bankrupt. The official receiver may allow you to use any bank or building society accounts that you have although your lenders may take a different view. You'll probably have to operate from a basic bank account without an overdraft. You cannot make any payment directly to your creditors. And in some cases, although it is unusual, you may have to appear in court if there are any questions or problems. If you fail to cooperate, or make false statements, you are commiting a criminal offence, which could lead to you being fined, or worse.

During the term of your bankruptcy, you are legally bound to inform the official receiver if you come into any money, if your salary increases or if your financial circumstances change in any way. The penalties and restriction can be much harsher if the courts determine that your bankruptcy was the result of grossly negligent and irresponsible behaviour.

After the term, your bankruptcy should be discharged and you will be free from all of your debt obligations. This usually occurs one year after the court has issued a bankruptcy order but it could come sooner. However, the official receiver may object. The reason for objecting may be that he or she feels you haven't cooperated fully, suspects you've been doing work for cash or that you transferred assets into other people's names in order to hide them. The receiver can place a bankruptcy restriction order on you for up to 15 years. It's best, therefore, to cooperate fully and honestly in order to put this behind you.

Your bankruptcy order will appear on the individual Insolvency Register, held by the Insolvency Service, for five years, and it will remain in your credit report for at least six years. Even after this time, when applying for certain jobs or loans, such as mortgages, you may have to admit that you have been bankrupt if you are asked. Bankruptcy can therefore be a shadow that hangs over your life for years.

In Scotland, the legal process by which you are declared bankrupt is known as *sequestration*. Many of the terms and procedures differ, but the basic principles are the same. Here are a few key differences:

- You must be 'apparently insolvent', which occurs when a creditor has raised a legal action against you, such as a statutory demand, a charge for payment, an attachment order or a receiving order. In most cases, you have to wait for this to happen before you can seek sequestration.
- The fee for filing the petition is much lower and this may be all you are required to pay.
- Your debts must be more than £1,500, and you cannot have been sequestrated in the last five years.
- Supplying false information on your application for sequestration can result in you being prosecuted. It's best to get legal advice.
- A trustee is appointed rather than an official receiver, but the role is the same.

After a bankruptcy it is crucially important that you organise your financial life, prioritise your goals and handle your money more prudently in order to avoid repeating the actions that got you into such a difficult situation in the first place. Going bankrupt isn't pretty and it's not the way you want to describe yourself, despite the celebrities who have recently been declared bankrupt. It is, however, a way to wipe the red ink from your finances and begin anew. You owe it to yourself to break the attitudes and cycle of habits that caused the problem. It is your second chance.

7 | HELP FROM YOURSELF AND OTHERS

The stigma of being in debt and having money problems is not what it used to be even a decade ago. If you tell your friends and family that you have money worries, they may be able to help in lots of ways, especially emotionally. However, I really don't recommend borrowing money from a relative when you have severe financial problems. If you are unable to pay back this money, the resulting anger and disappointment can cause an irreparable riff in your relationship. It is far better to look at family and friends as sources of emotional support.

Do not sugarcoat the problem, especially when talking with your immediate family. People are far more resourceful than you may be able to see given your own emotions at the time. Maybe your non-working spouse will realise that he or she has to go back to work and bring in a second wage to help the family get through this difficult time. Maybe your adult children will stop expecting you to spend money on meals, entertainment and gifts for them and for your grandchildren. Maybe friends will start inviting you over for dinner instead of asking you to a local restaurant that you really can't afford. Maybe family members will start giving you cash instead of presents at birthdays and Christmas, in order to help you through this time. Indeed, being so open may hurt your pride as a provider and as a person who has always tried to be responsible, but it may be just the support you need to begin to see the light at the end of what can appear to be a very dark tunnel of debt.

If you really cannot face telling your loved ones and close friends, visit your GP and ask to be referred to a counsellor with whom you can talk through the feelings – guilt, shame, anger, despair and hopelessness – that have arisen because of your money problems. You must talk about these feelings and realise that they are only temporary. Ultimately you never want to feel that you have to face your debt problems alone.

Free Help and Advice

If you can't create a plan of your own and need professional help in doing so and negotiating a deal with your creditors, the best place to start is one of the free debt counselling services available to everyone in the UK, regardless of your financial background. These government-sponsored or charitable agencies offer a wide array of professional services and can help you realistically assess your current situation, identify specific problems, help you create a budget and a debt-repayment plan, and negotiate with your creditors on your behalf. I think the counsellors, many of them volunteers, at these agencies know how to do their jobs very well and are dedicated to helping you solve your financial problems. However, you, the person in debt, must be honest and totally open with them about your situation. By giving them all of your financial details, you give them the tools to help you most effectively. With-holding important information because you're embarrassed, remembering at a later date a few debts you 'forgot' and failing to disclose the full extent of your financial situation hampers their ability to provide you with the quality service you need. By not making full and fair disclosure, you are, at the bottom line, sabotaging yourself. When you go to one of these companies, you are establishing a partnership, a working relationship, with someone who is there to help you, not hurt you and not judge you. Leave your scepticism at the door. Establishing a good rapport and clear line of communication with this person can only benefit you in your struggle to get out of debt. You won't be alone with these problems any more.

Citizens Advice Bureau (CAB)

The Citizens Advice Bureau is a government-funded charitable organisation that assists people in solving financial, legal and other problems. Using a staff of trained volunteers as counsellors, the CAB offers independent and confidential assistance to help you solve your specific financial and legal problems. You can access their services by visiting their offices located in nearly every city and town, or contacting them by phone or email (www.citizensadvice.org.uk). Some offices even offer home visits.

Citizens Advice will work out a debt-repayment plan for you, and they can negotiate with creditors on your behalf. They will also provide legal advice and assistance if you are being taken to court. Once they've worked out the deal, it is your responsibility to keep your side of the bargain and make the agreed repayments on time. There is no charge at all for the CAB's services. However, given the number of people across the UK who are having financial and debt problems today, you might find that you have to wait for an appointment with one of their counsellors, so don't wait until the last minute to ask for the CAB's assistance.

Consumer Credit Counselling Service (CCCS)

Another charitable organisation that offers independent and confidential debt counselling is the Consumer Credit Counselling Service. Unlike the CAB, the CCCS only offers help to people with debt problems and it does most of its counselling via a freephone telephone service (0800 138 1111). Its well-trained up-to-date counsellors can help you with a realistic assessment of your current financial situation, with personal budgeting and with developing a manageable debt-repayment plan, and can help you learn how to use credit wisely instead of destructively. They will negotiate directly with your creditor to freeze the interest on your debts, stop enforcing penalties and accept a longer period of repayment, among other things. As with the CAB, the CCCS counsellors do not charge for their work and take great pride in creating debt-management programmes that are both realistic and sustainable. Their website address is www.cccs.co.uk.

National Debtline
Part of the Money Advice Trust, a registered charity, the National Debtline offers a free telephone service for people throughout the UK (0808 808 4000). It provides callers with packs of information and fact sheets designed to enable them to get out of debt. It works with the government, private sector companies and other debt advice agencies like the Citizens Advice Bureau. It also has separate advice for people in Scotland that takes into account the difference in legislation. Users of the website (www.nationaldebtline.co.uk) will also find dozens of sample letters to creditors that can be used for different situations.

FCL Debt Clinic
FCL offers a freephone service that not only provides general debt-management and mortgage advice, but also helps to

arrange debt consolidation, repayment plans and individual voluntary arrangements, and advises about bankruptcy and other legal actions (0800 917 7823). Counsellors also help individuals correct and improve their credit reports. As with the National Debtline, FCL Debt Clinic works with other debt advice organisations like the Citizens Advice Bureau. It offers an online debt calculator that helps you understand the reality of your indebtedness (www.fcl.org.uk).

Credit Action

Credit Action is a national money-education charity that is closely affiliated with the Consumer Credit Counselling Service and with churches across the UK. This organisation regularly holds seminars in churches to teach people good money-management skills and how to avoid the pain of being in too much debt. It places a strong emphasis on self-help. Visit their website at www.creditaction.org.uk.

The organisations above are just some of the companies that offer free help for people who are having debt problems. The last three organisations offer primarily self-help advice. You can obtain one of their self-help packs via their websites or you can request it by calling them direct. When you fill out their self-assessment forms, the companies will use the information you provide to calculate the debt repayments you can afford and will put together a financial statement for you to use when you negotiate with your creditors. If you request one of these companies to create a debt-management plan for you, examine it carefully before you start contacting creditors yourself or letting the organisation do so on your behalf. You must be certain that you can stick to the plan and make the promised payments.

If you're involved in court procedures, the court will tell you how you can find someone to represent and advise you. Alternatively, the Legal Services Commission has several useful free leaflets (including one called 'Seeking Legal Help') and a useful website (www.legalservices.gov.uk).

The Six Golden Rules for Staying Out of Debt

Here are six tried-and-true pieces of advice and wisdom that have helped people not only get out of debt, but stay out. Each idea or concept is vital to your continued financial health and well-being. Choose the ones that will work best for you and integrate them into your daily life. Recommend those that are appropriate for family and friends who may be struggling with too much debt or with their finances in general. The goal is not only to remove the stress of indebtedness from all of our lives today and for ever, but to make staying this way a seamless part of our ongoing life activities.

1. *Know the truth in the numbers: don't spend what you don't have.* You have to see the total picture of your financial situation in order to formulate a way out of debt and then to keep it on track. Stop compartmentalising your finances – for example, stop viewing your mortgage as separate from your savings and both of those as separate from your debts. You must look realistically at what the numbers – i.e. the money that flows through your hands – tell you about the allocation of your income, your spending, your indebtedness and, once you've got out of debt, what you can realistically do with your money. This helps you get – and keep – your head out of the sand, take off your blinkers and, again, decompartmentalise your thinking about your finances.

   One of your mantras becomes 'If I don't have the money, then I won't spend.' This is age-old, commonsense advice. Be diligent and firm with yourself about keeping your outgoings less than your income. If you know the full map of your finances, you will not only have a clearer vision of where you are, but increase the likelihood of sustained and ever-increasing success in the battle among your income, your spending and your long-term goals for financial peace of mind.

2. *Stop victimising yourself.* Getting out of debt is more than just a game of getting the numbers in their proper balance. It is also a matter of getting yourself in balance – especially those desires that got you into this situation in the first place. Let's

be honest. Yes, the credit and shop solicitations that come through the post are tempting and will continue to be. So are the banks' offers of low-interest loans and the debt-management companies' offers for easy, pain-free repayments. Offers are one thing; accepting them is another. If you accepted the offers, then you are a victim of your own actions, not those of the bank, credit-card companies, the loan companies or other entities you may want to blame. You have done this to yourself. This is the first admission you must make.

The second issue you need to tackle is why. Why do you have such a problem with controlling your spending and handling your debts? For most of us, the problem arises from one of three sources. (An inability to understand numbers and maths is rarely one of them, although it is an excuse that is frequently put forth.) The three causes are 1) a sense of entitlement, 2) an inability to distinguish between one's 'needs' and 'wants' and 3) a desire to have a materially perfect life *now*.

People who have a sense of entitlement frequently use the word 'deserve' – 'I deserve this', 'You deserve to treat yourself.' Their other favourite phrase is 'I should be able to . . .' Do either of these describe you or someone you know? One way to get yourself out of this mindset is to ask yourself what have you done in your day-to-day life that has been exceptional and therefore worthy of special praise or treatment. If the honest answer is nothing, then you're spending money as a misleading form of therapy. Look inside yourself and find out what that need is. And then work hard to stop using it as the excuse for entitling yourself to spend.

'I've just got to have it' is a phrase that often pours from the lips of someone who blurs the line between 'want' and 'need'. They like the feeling of being propelled by the desire to buy something, as if it is the cosmic retail fates or some kind of retail intuition telling them that the object is meant to be theirs. They believe that if it feels right, they should do it. Never mind the consequences on the budget. To stop this impulsive behaviour, use the advice I gave you earlier – ask yourself, 'Do I really need this? Do I really need this?' Repeat the phrase several times, if necessary. You will be surprised how frequently your answer is no. This is your prompt to take control of yourself: admire the object and then walk away with your money still in *your* possession.

You must always be aware of the emotions that have driven you to overspend. For most of us, they don't go away. They always lurk in our lives, although we can control them. Only by recognising them and knowing the situations that stimulate them will you have a way to control your emotions and therefore your spending. In short, you have to learn how to stop yourself. This is essential in helping you take control of the flow of money through your life and to stop being your own worst financial nemesis.

3. *Plan more of your purchases.* This rule should apply to everything from your weekly food shop to major purchases (like cars, holidays and home improvements) to Christmas dinner and presents. During my years of advising people on *Your Money or Your Life* one of the biggest wastes of money we found in most people's budgets came when they shopped for food. Lots of people buy food impulsively thinking they will cook it; instead it ends up in the bin. By planning your visits to the supermarket carefully, making a list before you go shopping, and taking advantage of special offers each week, you can save anywhere from 10–20% of the money you normally spend on food. Turn to pages 31–2 for more detail.

   Prioritise and plan how you will save for big-ticket purchases, like new furniture, painting and decorating, a move to a new house. It's better to save money to cover the expenditure beforehand rather than taking out a loan. There's nothing wrong with a little delayed gratification. Often it is more exciting and satisfying to achieve a goal that you've decided is important to you without going into debt. In essence, the achievement is the reward for your sacrifice.

4. *Simplify your finances.* Many people have this concept that in order to be financially savvy you must be constantly doing something with your money. This is what causes them to start leveraging their lives – getting a home-equity loan, buying a rental apartment with that equity, getting a 0% credit card to buy the furniture, then getting another card

to cover those unexpected expenses that always seem to occur. And of course your lifestyle must reflect your perceived financial status, so your cost of living begins to increase. Soon you begin to feel overwhelmed by both the numbers and the quantity of statements for credit cards, store cards, unsecured loans and bank accounts. When you start to feel that way, close some of the accounts and consolidate others. The simpler your financial life, the easier it will be to keep track of all the things you must take care of and to monitor your progress toward your goals. You don't always have to get the best deal on this earth. Be happy with a very good deal. Be content that you know how your money is growing. Be pleased that you have not so overextended yourself that you are having sleepless nights. And don't feel the need to be one step too clever in order to show others just how savvy you may be or, even worse, how savvy you think you should be.

5. *Make your money work smarter for you.* It is important to get the best mortgage rate that you can, to avoid all of the bank fees that you can (such as charges for exceeding your overdraft limit), to pay the lowest interest on any outstanding credit-card debt you may have and to avoid all of those fees credit-card and store-card companies now routinely charge.

   'Avoiding' is just part of the picture of making your money work smarter for you. The other part is 'getting'. In these times of competition for your money and business as a consumer, you can get some very good deals. It starts with making sure you are getting a competitive, high interest rate on any money you have in savings. Be proactive in dealing with your bank or bank manager on this issue. Educate yourself about what's available and don't be afraid to ask your bank if they have an account that will match that of a competitor.

Learn how to make your money work twice for you. Like them or hate them, the new credit cards give you this ability. If you can use a credit card responsibly (which means paying off your entire balance at the end of every month), then the perks you receive from certain credit-card issuers are not only a reward, but they enable you to benefit a second time from the money you've already spent. Get a credit card that offers you Air Miles on your favourite airlines or hotel points at places you like to stay when on holiday, that gives you discounts in stores where you regularly shop, or contribute a percentage of the purchase price of certain items to your savings account. Again, if you can use a credit card wisely, in essence treating it like cash, it can provide you with benefits that are better than using real cash.

Consider investing part of your money in other assets, like stocks and shares, which can over the long term provide a higher return than other types of assets. But only invest after you've made sure all of your basic needs are covered. Shares are not for everyone. If you are uncomfortable with the idea, especially the risk, then don't invest. Make your money work smarter with what you know and what you are most comfortable with.

6. *Spend time with your money.* You may never find it fascinating, but managing your income, your outgoings and staying out of debt is far less trouble than getting out of debt, as this little book has shown. Take pride in your ability to balance your books, save money and make it work beneficially toward your long-term goals, but keep money in its place. It's a means to an end rather than an end in itself. Money can't always buy you happiness, but debt will always bring you unhappiness. Think of money management as an essential skill you need in order to enjoy life, doing whatever it is you want to do, in the place you like to be and surrounded by the people you love most.

Throughout the writing of this book, I have often thought of people I've met in the UK and the US over the years who have told me about their struggle with too much debt, who have taken control of the situation, creating a realistic, sustainable debt-management plan, and who have come through this difficult period with a renewed respect for money and debt, as well as an uplifting self-confidence in their ability to make their financial futures better.

There is a common thread in each of the stories and it is one that each person finds astonishing: that handling your personal finances responsibly, which had been viewed as a burden, is actually a source of freedom. Being out of debt, knowing where your money is going and continually developing an understanding of the choices and options available to you, enable to you to more easily steer life and ambitions in the direction that you want. You are the captain of your ship. Stay on your debt-free course to the financial security you desire. You can do it.

Index